THE BOLSHEVIKI
AND
WORLD PEACE

LECTOR HOUSE PUBLIC DOMAIN WORKS

THE BOLSHEVIKI AND WORLD PEACE

LEON TROTZKY,
LINCOLN STEFFENS

ISBN: 978-93-5420-882-9

Published: 1918

LECTOR HOUSE LLP
E-MAIL: lectorpublishing@gmail.com

Leon Trotzky

THE BOLSHEVIKI
AND
WORLD PEACE

BY

LEON TROTZKY

INTRODUCTION BY
LINCOLN STEFFENS

1918

CONTENTS

INTRODUCTION BY LINCOLN STEFFENS

The voice that speaks in this book is the voice of Leon Trotzky, the Bolshevik Minister of Foreign Affairs for Revolutionary Russia. It is expressing ideas and views which lighted him on the course of his policy toward the War, Peace and the Revolution. It throws light, therefore, on that policy; it helps to an understanding of it, if one wishes to understand. But that isn't all. The spirit that flames and casts shadows upon these pages is not only Trotzky's. It is the spirit also of the Bolsheviki; of the red left of the left wing of the revolutionary movement of New Russia. It flashed from Petrograd to Vladivostok, in the first week of the revolt; it burned all along the Russian Front before Trotzky appeared on the scene. It will smoulder long after he is gone. It is a hot Fact which has to be picked up and examined, this spirit. Whether we like it or don't, it is there; in Russia; it is elsewhere; it is everywhere to-day. It is the spirit of war; class war, but war. It is in this book.

Nor is that all.

The mind in this book--the point of view from which it starts, the views to which it points--Trotzky's mind is the international mind. We have heard before of this new intelligence; we have read books, heard speeches, witnessed acts demonstrative of thoughts and feelings which are not national, but international; not patriotic, but loyal only to the lower-class-conscious war aims of the workers of the world. The class warrior is as familiar a figure to us as the red spirit is of the red left of revolution. But the voice which utters here the spirit and the mind, not only of the Russian, but of the world revolution is the voice of one having authority.

And Trotzky, in power, has been as red as he is in this book. The minister of foreign affairs practised in Petrograd what he preached in Switzerland, where he wrote most of the chapters of his book. And he practised also what all the other great International Socialist leaders talked and wrote.

That's what makes him so hard to understand, him and his party and the Bolshevik policy. We are accustomed to the sight of Socialists and Radicals going into office and being "sobered by the responsibilities of power." French and Italian Socialists in the Liberal ministries of their countries; British Labor leaders in Parliament in England or in the governments of their Colonies; and the whole Socialist party in Germany and Austria (except Liebknecht in prison)--all are examples of the effect of power upon the International Mind. The phenomenon of compromise and surrender is so common that many radicals oppose the taking of any responsible office by any member of their parties; and some of the extremists are advocating no political action whatsoever, nothing but industrial, economic or what they call "direct action." (Our I.W.W.'s don't vote, on principle.) This is anarchism.

Leon Trotzky is not an anarchist; except in the ignorant sense of the word as used by educated people. He is a Socialist; an orthodox Marxian Socialist. But he has seen vividly the danger of political power. The body of this book was addressed originally to the German and Austrian Socialists, and it is a reasoned, but indignant reproach of them for letting their political position and their nationalistic loyalty carry them away into an undemocratic, patriotic, political policy which betrayed the weaker nations in their empires, helped break up the Second (Socialist) International and led the Socialist parties into the support of the War.

Clear upon it, Trotzky himself does not illustrate his own thesis. He not only detests intellectually the secrecy and the sordid wickedness of the "old diplomacy"; when he came as minister into possession of the archives of the Russian Foreign Office, he published the secret treaties.

That hurt. And so with the idea of a people's peace. All the democratic world had been talking ever since the war began of a peace made, not by diplomats in a private room, but by the chosen representatives of all the peoples meeting in an open congress. The Bolsheviki worked for that from the moment the Russian Revolution broke; and they labored for the Stockholm Conference while Paul Milyoukov and Alexander Kerensky were negotiating with the allied governments. When the Bolsheviki succeeded to power, Lenine and Trotzky formally authorized and officially proposed such a congress. Moreover Trotzky showed that they were willing, if they could, to force the other countries to accept the people's peace conference.

This hurt. This hurt so much that the governments united in extraordinary measures to prevent the event. And when they succeeded, and it was seen that no people's peace could be made openly and directly, Trotzky proceeded by another way to get to the same end. He opened negotiations with the Kaiser's government and allies; arranged an armistice and agreed tentatively upon terms of peace.

This act not only hurt; it stunned the world, and no wonder! It was like a declaration of war against a whole world at war. It was unbelievable. The only explanation offered was that Trotzky and Lenine were pro-German or dishonest, or both, and these things were said in high places; and they were said with conviction, too. Moreover this conviction colored, if it did not determine, the attitude the Allies took toward New Russia and the peace proposals Trotzky got from the German government. Was this assumption of the dishonesty of Trotzky the only explanation of his act?

This book shows, as I have said, that Trotzky saw things from the revolutionary, international point of view, which is not that of his judges; which is incomprehensible to them. He wrote it after the War began; he finished the main part of it before the Russian Revolution. It is his view of the War, its causes and its effects, especially upon international Socialism and "the" Revolution. These are the things he holds in his mind all through all these pages: "the" Revolution and world democracy. Also I have shown that, like the Russians generally, his mind is literal. The Russians mean what they say, exactly; and Trotzky not only means, he does what he writes. Putting these considerations together, we can make a comprehensible statement of the motive and the purpose of his policy; if we want to comprehend.

To all the other secretaries of state or of foreign affairs in the world, the Russian Revolution was an incident, an interruption of the War. To Minister Trotzky it was the other way around.

The World War was an incident, an effect, a check of "the" Revolution. Not the Russian Revolution, you understand. To Trotzky the Russian Revolution is but one, the first of that series of national revolutions which together will become the Thing he yearns for and prophesies: the World Revolution.

His peace policy therefore is a peace drive directed, not at a separate peace with the Central Powers; and not even at a general peace, but to an ending of the War in and by "the" Revolution everywhere.

Especially in Germany· and Austria. He said this. The correspondent of the London *Daily News* cabled on January 2, right after the armistice and the agreement upon peace terms to be offered the Allies, that "Trotzky is doing his utmost to stimulate a revolution in Germany.... Our only chance to defeat German designs is to publish terms (from the Allies) ... to help the democratic movement in Germany."

Trotzky is not pro-German. He certainly was not when he wrote this book. He hates here both the Austrian and the German dynasties, and his ill-will toward the House of Hapsburg is so bitter that it sounds sometimes as if there were something personal about it. And there is. He shows a knowledge of and a living sympathy with the small and subject nations which Austria rules, exploits and mistreats. He blames his Austrian comrades for their allegiance to a throne which is not merely undemocratic, but "senile" and tyrannical. That he, the literal Trotzky, would turn right around and, as the Russian Minister of Foreign Affairs, do what he had so recently criticized the Austrian Socialists for doing is unlikely.

Trotzky is against all the present governments of Europe, and the "bourgeois system" everywhere in the world. He isn't pro-Allies; he isn't even pro-Russian. He isn't a patriot at all. He is for a class, the proletariat, the working people of all countries, and he is for his class only to get rid of classes and get down or up to--humanity. And so with his people.

The Russians have listened to the Socialist propaganda for generations now. They have learned the chief lessons it has taught: liberty, land, industrial democracy and the class-war the world over. This War was not their war; it was the Czar's war; a war of the governments in the interest of their enemies, the capitalists of their several countries, who, as Trotzky says, were forcing their states to fight for the right to exploit other and smaller peoples. So when they overthrew the Czar, the Russians wanted to drop his war and go into their own, the class war. Kerensky held them at the front in the name of "the" Revolution; he would get peace for them by arrangement with the allies. He didn't; he couldn't; he was dismissed by them. Not by the Bolsheviki, but by the Russian people who know the three or four things they want: land and liberty at home; the Revolution and Democracy for all the world.

I heard a radical assert one day that that was the reason Trotzky could be such an exception to the rule about radicals in power. He came to the head of the Russian Revolution when his ideas were the actual demands of the Russian people and that it was not his strength of character, but the force of a democratic public opinion in mob power, which made him stick to his philosophy and carry out his theories and promises. I find upon inquiry here in New York that while he was living and working as a journalist on the East Side, he left one paper after another because he could not conform, to their editorial policies and would not compromise. He was "stiff-necked," "obstinate," "unreasonable." In other, kinder words, Trotzky is a strong man, with a definite mind and a purpose of his own, which he has the will and the nerve to pursue.

Also, however, Trotzky is a strong man who is ruled by and represents a very simple-minded people who are acting like him, literally upon the theory that the people govern now, in Russia; the common people; and that, since they don't like the War of the Czar, the Kaiser, the Kings and the Emperors, their government should make peace with the peoples of the world, a democratic peace against imperialism and capitalism and the state everywhere, for the establishment in its stead of a free, world-wide democracy.

That may be the true explanation of Trotzky's Bolshevik peace policy in the world crisis of the World War. That is the explanation which is suggested by this book.

"Written in extreme haste," he says at the close of his preface, "under conditions far from favorable to systematic work ... the entire book, from the first page to the last, was written with the idea of the New International constantly in mind--the New International which must rise out of the present world cataclysm, the International of the last conflict and the final victory."

LINCOLN STEFFENS.

New York, January 4th, 1918

AUTHOR'S PREFACE

The forces of production which capitalism has evolved have outgrown the limits of nation and state. The national state, the present political form, is too narrow for the exploitation of these productive forces. The natural tendency of our economic system, therefore, is to seek to break through the state boundaries. The whole globe, the land and the sea, the surface as well as the interior, has become one economic workshop, the different parts of which are inseparably connected with each other. This work was accomplished by capitalism. But in accomplishing it the capitalist states were led to struggle for the subjection of the world-embracing economic system to the profit interests of the bourgeoisie of each country. What the politics of imperialism has demonstrated more than anything else is that the old national state that was created in the revolutions and the wars of 1789-1815, 1848-1859, 1864-1866, and 1870 has outlived itself, and is now an intolerable hindrance to economic development.

The present War is at bottom a revolt of the forces of production against the political form of nation and state. It means the collapse of the national state as an independent economic unit.

The nation must continue to exist as a cultural, ideologic and psychological fact, but its economic foundation has been pulled from under its feet. All talk of the present bloody clash being a work of national defense is either hypocrisy or blindness. On the contrary, the real, objective significance of the war is the breakdown of the present national economic centres, and the substitution of a world economy in its stead. But the way the governments propose to solve this problem of imperialism is not through the intelligent, organized coöperation of all of humanity's producers, but through the exploitation of the world's economic system by the capitalist class of the victorious country; which country is by this War to be transformed from a great power into the world power.

The War proclaims the downfall of the national state. Yet at the same time it proclaims the downfall of the capitalist system of economy. By means of the national state capitalism has revolutionized the whole economic system of the world. It has divided the whole earth among the oligarchies of the great powers, around which were grouped the satellites, the small nations, who lived off the rivalry between the great ones. The future development of world economy on the capitalistic basis means a ceaseless struggle for new and ever new fields of capitalist exploitation, which must be obtained from one and the same source, the earth. The economic rivalry under the banner of militarism is accompanied by robbery and destruction which violate the elementary principles of human economy. World production revolts not only against the confusion produced by national and state divisions but also against the capitalist economic organization, which has now turned into barbarous disorganization and chaos.

The War of 1914 is the most colossal breakdown in history of an economic system destroyed by its own inherent contradictions.

All the historical forces whose task it has been to guide the bourgeois society, to speak in its name and to exploit it, have declared their historical bankruptcy by the War. They defended capitalism as a system of human civilization, and the catastrophe born out of that system is primarily *their* catastrophe. The first wave of events raised the national governments and armies to unprecedented heights never attained before. For the moment the nations rallied around them. But the more terrible will be the crash of the governments when the people, deafened by the thunder of the cannon, realize the meaning of the events now taking place in all their truth and frightfulness.

The revolutionary reaction of the masses will be all the more powerful the more prodigious the cataclysm which history is now bringing upon them.

Capitalism has created the material conditions of a new Socialist economic system. Imperialism has led the capitalist nations into historic chaos. The War of 1914 shows the way out of this chaos by violently urging the proletariat on to the path of Revolution.

For the economic backward countries of Europe the War brings to the fore problems of a far earlier historic origin--problems of democracy and national unity. This is in a large measure the case with the peoples of Russia, Austria-Hungary and the Balkan Peninsula. But these historically belated questions, which were bequeathed to the present epoch as a heritage from the past, do not alter the fundamental character of the events. It is not the national aspirations of the Serbs, Poles, Roumanians or Finns that has mobilized twenty-five million soldiers and placed them in the battlefields, but the imperialistic interests of the bourgeoisie of the Great Powers. It is imperialism that has upset completely the European *status quo*, maintained for forty-five years, and raised again the old questions which the bourgeois revolution proved itself powerless to solve.

Yet in the present epoch it is quite impossible to treat these questions in and by themselves. They are utterly devoid of an independent character. The creation of normal relations of national life and economic development on the Balkan Peninsula is unthinkable if Czarism and Austria-Hungary are preserved. Czarism is now the indispensable military reservoir for the financial imperialism of France and the conservative colonial power of England. Austria-Hungary is the mainstay of Germany's imperialism. Issuing from the private family clashes between the national Servian terrorists and the Hapsburg political police, the War very quickly revealed its true fundamental character--a struggle of life and death between Germany and England. While the simpletons and hypocrites prate of the defense of national freedom and independence, the German-English War is really being waged for the freedom of the imperialistic exploitation of the peoples of India and

Egypt on the one hand, and for the imperialistic division of the peoples of the earth on the other.

Germany began its capitalistic development on a national basis with the destruction of the continental hegemony of France in the year 1870-1871. Now that the development of German industry on a national foundation has transformed Germany into the first capitalistic power of the world, she finds herself colliding with the hegemony of England in her further course of development. The complete and unlimited domination of the European continent seems to Germany the indispensable prerequisite of the overthrow of her world enemy. The first thing, therefore, that imperialistic Germany writes in her programme is the creation of a Middle European League of Nations. Germany, Austria-Hungary, the Balkan Peninsula and Turkey, Holland, the Scandinavian countries, Switzerland, Italy, and, if possible, enfeebled France and Spain and Portugal, are to make one economic and military whole, a Great Germany under the hegemony of the present German state.

This programme, which has been thoroughly elaborated by the economists, political students, jurists and diplomats of German imperialism and translated into reality by its strategists, is the most striking proof and most eloquent expression of the fact that capitalism has expanded beyond the limits of the national state and feels intolerably cramped within its boundaries. The national Great Power must go and in its place must step the imperialistic World Power.

In these historical circumstances the working class, the proletariat, can have no interest in defending the outlived and antiquated national "fatherland," which has become the main obstacle to economic development. The task of the proletariat is to create a far more powerful fatherland, with far greater power of resistance--*the republican United States of Europe*, as the foundation of the United States of the World.

The only way in which the proletariat can meet the imperialistic perplexity of capitalism is by opposing to it as a practical programme of the day the Socialist organization of world economy.

War is the method by which capitalism, at the climax of its development, seeks to solve its insoluble contradictions. To this method the proletariat must oppose its *own* method, the method of the Social Revolution.

The Balkan question and the question of the overthrow of Czarism, propounded to us by the Europe of yesterday, can be solved only in a revolutionary way, in connection with the problem of the United Europe of to-morrow. The immediate, urgent task of the Russian Social Democracy, to which the author belongs, is the fight against Czarism. What Czarism primarily seeks in Austria-Hungary and the Balkans is a market for its political methods of plunder, robbery and acts of violence. The Russian bourgeoisie all the way up to its radical intellectuals has become completely demoralized by the tremendous growth of industry in the last five years, and it has entered into a bloody league with the dynasty, which had to secure to the impatient Russian capitalists their part of the world's booty by new land robberies. While Czarism stormed and devastated Galicia, and deprived it even of the rags and tatters of liberty granted to it by the Hapsburgs, while it dismembered unhappy Persia, and from the corner of the Bosporus strove to throw the noose around the neck of the Balkan peoples, it left to the liberalism which it despised the task of concealing its robbery by sickening declamations over the defense of Belgium and France. The year 1914 spells the complete bankruptcy of Russian liberalism, and makes the Russian proletariat the sole champion of the war of liberation. It makes the Russian Revolution definitely an integral part of the Social Revolution of the European proletariat.

In our war against Czarism, in which we have never known a "national" truce, we have never looked for help from Hapsburg or Hohenzollern militarism, and we are not looking for it now. We have preserved a sufficiently clear revolutionary vision to know that the idea of destroying Czarism was utterly repugnant to German imperialism. Czarism has been its best ally on the Eastern border. It is united to it by close ties of social structure and historical aims. Yet even if it were otherwise, even if it could be assumed that, in obedience to the logic of military operations, it would deal a destructive blow to Czarism, in defiance of the logic of its own political interests--even in such a highly improbable case we should refuse to regard the Hohenzollerns not only as an objective but as a subjective ally. The fate of the Russian Revolution is so inseparably bound up with the fate of European Socialism, and we Russian Socialists stand so firmly on the ground of internationalism, that we cannot, we must not for a moment, entertain the idea of purchasing the doubtful liberation of Russia by the certain destruction of the liberty of Belgium and France, and--what is more important still--thereby inoculating the German and Austrian proletariat with the virus of imperialism.

We are united by many ties to the German Social Democracy. We have all gone through the German Socialist school, and learned lessons from its successes as well as from its failures. The German Social Democracy was to us not only *a* party of the International. It was *the* Party *par excellence*. We have always preserved and fortified the fraternal bond that united us with the Austrian Social Democracy. On the other hand, we have always taken pride in the fact that we have made our modest contribution towards winning suffrage in Austria and arousing revolutionary tendencies in the German working class. It cost more than one drop of blood to do it. We have unhesitatingly accepted moral and material support from our older brother who fought for the same ends as we on the other side of our Western border.

Yet it is just because of this respect for the past, and still more out of respect for the future, which ought to unite the working class of Russia with the working classes of Germany and Austria, that we indignantly reject the "liberating" aid which German imperialism offers us in a Krupp munition box, with the blessing, alas! of German Socialism. And we hope that the indignant protest of Russian Socialism will be loud enough to be heard in Berlin and in Vienna.

The collapse of the Second International is a tragic fact, and it were blindness or cowardice to close one's eyes to it. The position taken by the French and by the larger part of English Socialism is as much a part of this breakdown as the position of the German and Austrian Social Democracy. If the present work addresses itself chiefly to the German Social Democracy it is only because the German party was the strongest, most influential, and in principle the most basic member of the Socialist world. Its historic capitulation reveals most clearly the causes of the downfall of the Second International. At first glance it may appear that the social revolutionary prospects of the future are wholly deceptive. The insolvency of the old Socialist parties has become catastrophically apparent. Why should we have faith in the future of the Socialist movement? Such skepticism, though natural, nevertheless leads to quite an erroneous conclusion. It leaves out of account the good will of history, just as we have often been too prone to ignore its ill will, which has now so cruelly shown itself in the fate that has overcome the International.

The present War signalizes the collapse of the national states. The Socialist parties of the epoch now concluded were national parties. They had become ingrained in the national states with all the different branches of their organizations, with all their activities and with their psychology. In the face of the solemn declarations at their congresses they rose to the defense of the conservative state, when imperialism, grown big on the national soil, began to demolish the antiquated national barriers. And in their historic crash the national states have pulled down with them the national Socialist parties also.

It is not Socialism that has gone down, but its temporary historical external form. The revolutionary idea begins its life anew as it casts off its old rigid shell. This shell is made up of living human beings, of an entire generation of Socialists that has become fossilized in self-abnegating work of agitation and organization through a period of several decades of political reaction, and has fallen into the habits and views of national opportunism or possibilism. All efforts to save the Second International on the old basis, by personal diplomatic methods and mutual concessions, are quite hopeless. The old mole of history is now digging its passageways all too well and none has the power to stop him.

As the national states have become a hindrance to the development of the forces of production, so the old Socialist parties have become the main hindrance to the revolutionary movement of the working class. It was necessary that they should demonstrate to the full their extreme backwardness, that they should discredit their utterly inadequate and narrow methods, and bring the shame and horror of national discord upon the proletariat, in order that the working class might emancipate itself, through these fearful disillusionments, from the prejudices and slavish habits of the period of preparation, and become at last that which the voice of history is now calling it to be--the revolutionary class fighting for power.

The Second International has not lived in vain. It has accomplished a huge cultural work. There has been nothing like it in history before. It has educated and assembled the oppressed classes. The proletariat does not now need to begin at the beginning. It enters on the new road not with empty hands. The past epoch has bequeathed to it a rich arsenal of ideas. It has bequeathed to it the weapons of criticism. The new epoch will teach the proletariat to combine the old weapons of criticism with the new criticism of weapons.

This book was written in extreme haste, under conditions far from favorable to systematic work. A large part of it is devoted to the old International which has fallen. But the entire book, from the first to the last page, was written with the idea of the New International constantly in mind, the New International which must rise up out of the present world cataclysm, the International of the last conflict and the final victory.

LEON TROTZKY.

THE BOLSHEVIKI AND WORLD PEACE

CHAPTER I

THE BALKAN QUESTION

"The War at present being waged against Russian Czarism and its vassals is dominated by a great historic idea. The impetus of this great historic idea consecrates the battlefields of Poland and of Eastern Russia. The roar of cannon, the rattling of machine guns, and the onrush of cavalry, all betoken the enforcement of the democratic programme for the liberation of the nations. Had Czarism, in league with the French capitalistic powers and in league with an unscrupulous 'nation of shopkeepers,' not succeeded in suppressing the Revolution of 1905, the present slaughter of the nations would have been avoided.

"A democratic Russia would never have consented to wage this unscrupulous and futile War. The great ideas of freedom and justice now speak the persuasive language of the machine gun and the sword, and every heart susceptible of sympathy with justice and humanity can only wish that the power of Czarism may be destroyed once for all, and that the oppressed Russian nationalities may again secure the right to decide their own destinies."

The above quotation is from the *Nepszava* of August 31, 1914, the official organ of the Socialist party of Hungary. Hungary is the land whose entire inner life was erected upon the high-handed oppression of the national minorities, upon the enslavement of the laboring classes, upon the official parasitism and usury of the ruling caste of large landowners. It is the land in which men like Tisza are masters of the situation, dyed-in-the-wool agrarians, with the manners of political bandits. In a word, Hungary is a country closest of kin to Czar-ruled Russia.

So what is more fitting than that the *Nepszava*, the Socialist organ of Hungary, should hail with outbursts of enthusiasm the liberating mission of the German and Austro-Hungarian armies? Who other than Count Tisza could have felt the call to "enforce the democratic programme for the liberation of the nations"? Who was there to uphold the eternal principles of law and justice in Europe but the ruling clique of Budapest, the discredited Panamists? Would you entrust this mission to the unscrupulous diplomacy of "perfidious Albion," to the nation of shopkeepers?

Laughter turns away wrath. The tragic inconsistencies of the policies followed by the International not only reach their climax in the articles of the poor Nepszava; they disarm us by their humor.

The present series of events began with the ultimatum, sent to Servia by Austria-Hungary. There was not the slightest reason why the international Social Democracy should take under its protection the intrigues of the Serbs or any other of the petty dynasties of the Balkan Peninsula. They were all endeavoring to hide their political adventures under the cloak of national aspirations. We had still less cause to lash ourselves into a state of moral indignation because a fanatic young Serb responded to the cowardly, criminal and wily national politics of the Vienna and Budapest government authorities with a bloody assassination.[1]

Of one thing we have no doubt. In the dealings between the Danube Monarchy and the Servian government, the historic right, that is to say, the right of free development, rests entirely with Servia, just as Italy was in the right in the year 1859. Underneath the duel between the imperial police scoundrels and the terrorists of Belgrade, there is hidden a far deeper meaning than merely the greed of the Kareorgoievitches or the crimes of the Czar's diplomacy. On one side were the imperialistic claims of a national state that had lost its vitality, and on the other side, the strivings of the dismembered Servian nation to reintegrate itself into a national whole and become a living vital state.

Is it for this that we have sat so long in the school of Socialism to forget the first three letters of the democratic alphabet? This absolute lapse of memory, moreover, made its appearance only after the fourth of August. Up to that fatal date the German Marxists showed that they knew very well what was happening in Southeastern Europe.

On July 3, 1914, after the assassination at Sarajevo, the *Vorwärts* wrote:

> "The bourgeois revolution of the South Slavs is in full swing, and the shooting at Sarajevo, however wild and senseless an act in itself, is as much a chapter of this revolution as the battles by which the Bulgarians, Serbs and Montenegrins liberated the peasants of Macedonia from the yoke of Turkish feudal exploitation. Is it a wonder that the South Slavs of Austria-Hungary look with longing to their racial brothers in the kingdom of Servia? The Serbs in Servia have attained the highest goal a people can attain in the present order of society. They have attained national inde-

---

[1] It is noteworthy that these opportunistic Austrian and German Socialists are now writhing with moral indignation over the "treacherous assassination at Sarajevo." And yet they always sympathized with the Russian terrorists more than we, the Russian Social Democrats, did, who are opposed on principle to the terroristic method. Lost in the mist of chauvinism, they can no longer see that the unfortunate Servian terrorist, Gavrilo Prinzip, represents precisely the same national principle as the German terrorist, Sand. Perhaps they will even ask us to transfer our sympathies from Sand to Kotzebue? Or perhaps these eunuchs will advise the Swiss to overthrow the monuments erected to the assassin Tell and replace them with monuments to the Austrian governor, Gessler, one of the spiritual forerunners of the murdered archduke?

pendence. Whereas in Vienna or Budapest they treat every one bearing the name of Serb or Croatian with blows and kicks, with court-martial justice and the gallows.... There are seven and a half million South Slavs who, as a result of the victories in the Balkans, have grown bolder than ever in demanding their political rights. And if the imperial throne of Austria continues to resist their impact, it will topple over and the entire Empire with which we have coupled our destiny will break to pieces. For it is in line with historic evolution that such national revolutions should march onward to victory."

If the international Social Democracy together with its Servian contingent, offered unyielding resistance to Servia's national claims, it was certainly not out of any consideration for the historic rights of Austria-Hungary to oppress and disintegrate the nationalities living within her borders; and most certainly not out of consideration for the liberating mission of the Hapsburgs. Until August, 1914, no one, except the black and yellow hirelings of the press, dared to breathe a word about that. The Socialists were influenced in their course of conduct by entirely different motives. First of all, the proletariat, although by no means disputing the historic right of Servia to strive for national unity, could not trust the solution of this problem to the powers then controlling the destinies of the Servian kingdom. And in the second place--and this was for us the deciding factor--the international Social Democracy could not sacrifice the peace of Europe to the national cause of the Serbs, recognizing, as it did, that, except for a European revolution, the only way such unity could be achieved was through a European war.

But from the moment Austria-Hungary carried the question of her own fate and that of Servia to the battlefield, Socialists could no longer have the slightest doubt that social and national progress would be hit much harder in Southeastern Europe by a Hapsburg victory than by a Servian victory. To be sure, there was still no reason for us Socialists to identify our cause with the aims of the Servian army. This was the idea that animated the Servian Socialists, Ljaptchevitch and Katzlerovitch, when they took the manly stand of voting against the war credits.[2] But surely we had still less reason to support the purely dynastic rights of the

[2] To appreciate fully this action of the Servian Socialists we must bear in mind the political situation by which they were confronted. A group of Servian conspirators had murdered a member of the Hapsburg family, the mainstay of Austro-Hungarian clericalism, militarism, and imperialism. Using this as a welcome pretext, the military party in Vienna sent an ultimatum to Servia, which, for sheer audacity, has scarcely ever been paralleled in diplomatic history. In reply, the Servian government made extraordinary concessions, and suggested that the solution of the question in dispute be turned over to the Hague tribunal. Thereupon Austria declared war on Servia. If the idea of a "war of defense" has any meaning at all, it certainly applied to Servia in this instance. Nevertheless, our friends, Ljaptchevitch and Katzlerovitch, unshaken in their conviction of the course of action that they as Socialists must pursue, refused the government a vote of confidence. The writer was in Servia at the beginning of the War. In the Skuptchina, in an atmosphere of indescribable national enthusiasm, a vote was taken on the war credits. The voting was by roll-call. Two hundred members had all answered "Yes." Then in a moment of deathlike silence came the voice of the Socialist Ljaptchevitch--"No." Every one felt the moral force of this protest, and

Hapsburgs and the imperialistic interests of the feudal-capitalistic cliques against the national struggle of the Serbs. At all events, the Austro-Hungarian Social Democracy, which now invokes its blessings upon the sword of the Hapsburgs for the liberation of the Poles, the Ukrainians, the Finns and the Russian people, must first of all clarify its ideas on the Servian question, which it has gotten so hopelessly muddled.

The question at issue, however, is not confined to the fate of the ten million Serbs. The clash of the European nations has brought up the entire Balkan question anew. The Peace of Bucharest, signed in 1903, has solved neither the national nor the international problems in the Near East. It has only intensified the added confusion resulting from the two unfinished Balkan Wars, unfinished because of the complete temporary exhaustion of the nations participating in it.

Roumania had followed in the path of Austro-Hungarian politics, despite the Romanesque sympathies of its population, especially in the cities. This was due not so much to dynastic causes, to the fact that a Hohenzollern prince occupied the throne, as to the imminent danger of a Russian invasion. In 1879 the Russian Czar, as thanks for Roumania's support in the Russo-Turkish war of "liberation," cut off a slice of Roumanian territory, the province of Bessarabia. This eloquent deed provided a sufficient backing to the dynastic sympathies of the Hohenzollern in Bucharest. But the Magyar-Hapsburg clique succeeded in incensing the Roumanian people against them by their denationalizing policy in Transylvania, which has a population of three million Roumanians as against three-fourths of a million in the Russian province of Bessarabia; and they further antagonized them by their commercial treaties, which were dictated by the interests of the large Austro-Hungarian land-owners. So that Roumania's entrance into the War on the side of the Czar, despite the courageous and active agitation against participation in the War on either side, carried on by the Socialist party under the leadership of my friends Gherea and Rakowsky, is to be laid altogether at the door of the ruling class of Austria-Hungary, who are reaping the harvest they have sown here as well as elsewhere.

But the matter is not disposed of by fixing the historical responsibility. To-morrow, in a month, in a year or more the War will bring to the foreground the whole question of the destiny of the Balkan peoples and of Austria-Hungary, and the proletariat will have to have its answer to this question. European democracy in the nineteenth century looked with distrust at the Balkan people's struggle for independence, because it feared that Russia might be strengthened at the expense of Turkey. On this subject Karl Marx wrote in 1853, on the eve of the Crimean War:

> "It may be said that the more firmly established Servia and the Servian nationality is the more the direct influence of Russia on the Turkish Slavs is shoved into the background. For in order to be able to assert its peculiar position as a state, Servia had to import its political institutions, its schools ... from Western Europe."

This prophecy has been brilliantly fulfilled in what has actually happened in

---

the scene has remained indelibly impressed upon my memory.

Bulgaria, which was created by Russia as an outpost on the Balkans. As soon as Bulgaria was fairly well established as a national state, it developed a strong anti-Russian party, under the leadership of Russia's former pupil, Stambulov, and this party was able to stamp its iron seal upon the entire foreign policy of the young country. The whole mechanism of the political parties in Bulgaria is so constructed as to enable it to steer between the two European combinations without being absolutely forced into the channel of either, unless it chooses to enter it of its own accord. Roumania went with the Austro-German alliance, Servia, since 1903, with Russia, because the one was menaced directly by Russia, the other by Austria. The more independent the countries of Southeast Europe are from Austria-Hungary, the more effectively they will be able to protect their independence against Czarism.

The balance of power in the Balkans, created by the Congress of Berlin in 1879, was full of contradictions. Cut up by artificial ethnographical boundaries, placed under the control of imported dynasties from German nurseries, bound hand and foot by the intrigues of the Great Powers, the peoples of the Balkans could not cease their efforts for further national freedom and unity. The national politics of independent Bulgaria was naturally directed towards Macedonia, populated by Bulgarians. The Berlin Congress had left it under Turkish rule. On the other hand, Servia had practically nothing to look for in Turkey with the exception of the little strip of land, the sandbag Novy Bazar. Its national interests lay on the other side of the Austro-Hungarian boundary, in Bosnia-Herzegovina, Croatia, Slavonia and Dalmatia. Roumania had no interests in the south, where it is separated from European Turkey by Servia and Bulgaria. Roumania's expansion policy was directed towards the northwest and east, towards Hungarian Transylvania and Russian Bessarabia. Finally, the national expansion of Greece, like that of Bulgaria, collided with Turkey.

Austro-German politics, aiming at the artificial preservation of European Turkey, broke down not on account of the diplomatic intrigues of Russia, although these of course were not lacking. It broke down because of the inevitable course of evolution. The Balkan Peninsula had entered on the path of capitalist development, and it was this fact that raised the question of the self-determination of the Balkan peoples as national states to the historical issue of the day.

The Balkan War disposed of European Turkey, and thereby created the conditions necessary for the solution of the Bulgarian and Greek questions. But Servia and Roumania, whose national completion could only be achieved at the expense of Austria-Hungary, found themselves checked in their efforts at expansion southwards, and were compensated at the expense of what racially belonged to Bulgaria--Servia in Macedonia, and Roumania in Dobrudja. This is the meaning of the second Balkan War and the Peace of Bucharest by which it was concluded.

The mere existence of Austria-Hungary, this Turkey of Middle Europe, blocks the way to the natural self-determination of the peoples of the Southeast. It compels them to keep constantly fighting against each other, to seek support against each other from the outside, and so makes them the tool of the political combinations of the Great Powers. It was only in such chaos that Czaristic diplomacy was enabled to spin the web of its Balkan politics, the last thread of which was Constantinople. And only a federation of the Balkan states, both economic and military, can interpose an invincible barrier to the greed of Czarism.

Now that European Turkey has been disposed of, it is Austria-Hungary that stands in the way of a federation of the Balkan states. Roumania, Bulgaria, and Servia would have found their natural boundaries, and would have united with Greece and Turkey, on the basis of common economic interests, into a league of defense. This would finally have brought peace to the Balkan Peninsula, that witches' cauldron which periodically threatened Europe with explosions, until it drew it into the present catastrophe.

Up to a certain time the Socialists had to reconcile themselves to the routine way in which the Balkan question was treated by capitalistic diplomats, who in their conferences and secret agreements stopped up one hole only to open another, even wider one. So long as this dilatory method kept postponing the final solution, the Socialist International could hope that the settlement of the Hapsburg succession would be a matter not for a European war, but for the European Revolution. But now that the War has destroyed the equilibrium of the whole of Europe, and the predatory Powers are seeking to remodel the map of Europe--not on the basis of national democratic principles, but of military strength--the Social Democracy must come to a clear comprehension of the fact that one of the chief obstacles to freedom, peace and progress, in addition to Czarism and German militarism, is the Hapsburg Monarchy as a state organization. The crime of the Galician Socialist group under Daszynski consisted not only in placing the Polish cause above the cause of Socialism, but also in linking the fate of Poland with the fate of the Austro-Hungarian armies and the fate of the Hapsburg Monarchy.

The Socialist proletariat of Europe cannot adopt such a solution of the question. For us the question of united and independent Poland is on a par with the question of united and independent Servia. We cannot and we will not permit the Polish question to be solved by methods which will perpetuate the chaos at present prevailing in Southeastern Europe, in fact through the whole of Europe. For us Socialists the independence of Poland means its independence on both fronts, on the Romanoff front and on the Hapsburg front. We not only wish the Polish people to be free from the oppression of Czarism. We wish also that the fate of the Servian people shall not be dependent upon the Polish nobility in Galicia.

For the present we need not consider what the relations of an independent Poland will be to Bohemia, Hungary and the Balkan Federation. But it is perfectly clear that a complex of medium-sized and small states on the Danube and in the Balkan Peninsula will constitute a far more effective bar to the Czaristic designs on Europe than the weak, chaotic Austro-Hungarian State, which proves its right to existence only by its continued attempts upon the peace of Europe.

In the article of 1853, quoted above, Marx wrote as follows on the Eastern question:

> "We have seen that the statesmen of Europe, in their obdurate
> stupidity, petrified routine, and hereditary intellectual indolence,

recoil from every attempt at answering the question of what is to become of Turkey in Europe. The driving force that favors Russia's advance towards Constantinople is the very means by which it is thought to keep her away from it, the empty theory, never carried out, of maintaining the *status quo*. What is this *status quo*? For the Christian subjects of the Porte it means nothing else than the perpetuation of their oppression by Turkey. As long as they are under the yoke of the Turkish rule, they look upon the head of the Greek Church, the ruler of 60 million Greek Church Christians, as *their natural protector and liberator*."

What is here said of Turkey now applies in a still greater degree to Austria-Hungary. The solution of the Balkan question is unthinkable without the solution of the Austro-Hungarian question, as they are both comprised in one and the same formula--the Democratic Federation of the Danube and Balkan Nations.

"The governments with their old-fashioned diplomacy," wrote Marx, "will never solve the difficulty. Like the solution of so many other problems, the Turkish problem, too, is reserved for the European Revolution." This statement holds just as good to-day as when it was first written. But for the Revolution to solve the difficulties that have piled up in the course of centuries, the proletariat must have its *own* programme for the solution of the Austro-Hungarian question. And this programme it must oppose just as strenuously to the Czaristic greed of conquest as to the cowardly and conservative efforts to maintain the Austro-Hungarian *status quo*.

CHAPTER II

AUSTRIA-HUNGARY

Russian Czarism undoubtedly represents a cruder and more barbarian form of state organization than does the feebler absolutism of Austria-Hungary, which has been mitigated by the weakness of old age. But Russian Czarism and the Russian state are by no means identical. The destruction of Czarism does not mean the disintegration of the state. On the contrary it means its liberation and its strengthening. All such assertions, as that it is necessary to push Russia back into Asia, which found an echo even in certain Social Democratic organs, are based on a poor knowledge of geography and ethnography. Whatever may be the fate of various parts of present Russia--Russian Poland, Finland, the Ukraine or Bessarabia--European Russia will not cease to exist as the national territory of a many-millioned race that has made notable conquests along the line of cultural development during the last quarter century.

Quite different is the case of Austria-Hungary. As a state organization it is identical with the Hapsburg Monarchy. It stands or falls with the Hapsburgs, just as European Turkey was identical with the feudal-military Ottoman caste and fell when that caste fell. A conglomerate of racial fragments centrifugal in tendency, yet forced by a dynasty to stick together, Austria-Hungary presents the most reactionary picture in the very heart of Europe. Its continuation after the present European catastrophe would not only delay the development of the Danube and Balkan peoples for more decades to come and make a repetition of the present War a practical certainty, but it would also strengthen Czarism politically by preserving its main source of spiritual nourishment.

If the German Social Democracy reconciles itself to the ruin of France by regarding it as punishment for France's alliance with Czarism, then we must ask that the same criterion be applied to the German-Austrian alliance. And if the alliance of the two Western democracies with a despotic Czarism gives the lie to the French and English press when they represent the War as one of liberation, then is it not equally arrogant, if not more so, for the German Social Democracy to spread the banner of liberty over the Hohenzollern army, the army that is fighting not only *against* Czarism and its allies but also *for* the entrenchment of the Hapsburg Monarchy?

Austria-Hungary is indispensable to Germany, to the ruling class in Germany as we know it. When the ruling Junker class threw France into the arms of Czarism by the forceful annexation of Alsace-Lorraine, and systematically embittered the relations with England by rapidly increasing naval armaments; when it repulsed all attempts at an understanding with the Western democracies because such an understanding would have implied the democratization of Germany--then this ruling class saw itself compelled to seek support from the Austro-Hungarian Monarchy as a reserve source of military strength against the enemies in the East and the West.

According to the German point of view the mission of the Dual Monarchy was to place Hungarian, Polish, Roumanian, Czech, Ruthenian, Servian and Italian auxiliaries in the service of the German military and Junker policy. The ruling class in Germany had easily reconciled itself to the expatriation of ten to twelve millions of Germans, for these twelve millions formed the kernel around which the Hapsburgs united a non-German population of more than forty million. A democratic federation of independent Danube nations would have made these peoples useless as allies of German militarism. Only a monarchy, in Austria-Hungary, a monarchy enforced by militarism, would make that country of any value as an ally to Junker Germany. The indispensable condition for this alliance, sanctified by the Nibelungen troth of dynasties, was the military preparedness of Austria-Hungary, a condition to be achieved in no other way than by the mechanical suppression of the centrifugal national tendencies.

Since Austria-Hungary is surrounded on all sides by states composed of the same races as are within its own borders, its foreign policy is necessarily intimately connected with its internal policy. To keep seven million Serbs and South Slavs within the frame of its own military state, Austria-Hungary is compelled to extinguish the hearthfire that kindles their political leanings--the independent kingdom of Servia.

Austria's ultimatum to Servia was the decisive step in this direction. "Austria-Hungary took this step under the pressure of necessity," wrote Eduard Bernstein in *Die Sozialistische Monatshefte* (No. 16). To be sure it was, if political events are considered from the viewpoint of *dynastic* necessity.

To defend the Hapsburg policy on the ground of the low moral standard of the Belgrade rulers is to close one's eyes to the fact that the Hapsburgs did make friends with Servia, but only when Servia was under the most despicable government that the history of the unfortunate Balkan Peninsula has known, that is, when it had at its head an Austrian agent, Milan. The reckoning with Servia came so late because the efforts made at self-preservation were too weak in the enfeebled organism of the Dual Monarchy. But after the death of the Archduke, the support and hope of the Austrian military party--and of Berlin--Austria's ally gave her a sharp dig in the ribs, insisting upon a demonstration of firmness and strength. Not only was Austria's ultimatum to Servia approved of in advance by the rulers of Germany, but, according to all information, it was actually inspired from that quarter. The evidence is plainly set forth in the very same White Book which professional and amateur diplomats offer as a document of the Hohenzollern love of peace.

After defining the aims of Greater Servian propaganda and the machinations of Czarism in the Balkans, the White Book states:

> "Under such conditions Austria was forced to the realization that it was not compatible with the dignity or the self-preservation of the Monarchy to look on at the doings across the border and remain passive. The Imperial Government informed us of this view and asked for our opinion. We could sincerely tell our ally that we agreed with his estimate of the situation and could assure him that any action he might find necessary to put an end to the movement in Servia against the Austrian Monarchy would meet with our approval. In doing so, we were well aware of the fact that eventual war operations on the part of Austria-Hungary might bring Russia into the field and might, according to the terms of our alliance, involve us in a war.

> "But in view of the vital interests of Austria-Hungary that were at stake, we could not advise our ally to show a leniency incompatible with his dignity, or refuse him our support in a moment of such grave portent. We were the less able to do so because our own interests also were vitally threatened by the persistent agitation in Servia. If the Serbs, aided by Russia and France, had been allowed to go on endangering the stability of our neighboring Monarchy, this would have led to the gradual breakdown of Austria and to the subjection of all the Slavic races to the Russian rule. And this in turn would have made the position of the Germanic race in Central Europe quite precarious. An Austria morally weakened, breaking down before the advance of Russian Pan-Slavism, would not be an ally with whom we could reckon and on whom we could depend, as we are obliged to depend, in the face of the increasingly threatening attitude of our neighbors to the East and the West. We therefore left Austria a free hand in its action against Servia."

The relation of the ruling class in Germany to the Austro-Servian conflict is here fully and clearly defined. It is not merely that Germany was informed by the Austrian Government of the latter's intentions, not merely that she approved them, and not merely that she accepted the consequences of fidelity to an ally. No, Germany looked on Austria's aggression as unavoidable, as a saving act for herself, and actually made it *a condition of the continuance of the alliance*. Otherwise, "Austria would not be an ally with whom we could reckon."

The German Marxists were fully aware of this state of affairs and of the dangers lurking in it. On June 29th, a day after the murder of the Austrian Archduke, the *Vorwärts* wrote as follows:

> "The fate of our nation has been all too closely knit with that of Austria as a result of a bungling foreign policy. Our rulers have made the alliance with Austria the basis of our entire foreign policy. Yet it becomes clearer every day that this alliance is a source of

weakness rather than of strength. The *problem of Austria* threatens more and more to become a *menace to the peace of Europe.*"

A month later, when the menace was about to culminate in the dread actuality of war, on July 28th, the chief organ of the German Social Democracy wrote in equally definite terms. "How shall the German proletariat act in the face of such a senseless paroxysm?" it asked; and then gave the answer: *"The German proletariat is not in the least interested in the preservation of the Austrian national chaos."*

Quite the contrary. Democratic Germany is far more interested in the disruption than in the preservation of Austria-Hungary. A disrupted Austria-Hungary would mean a gain to Germany of an educated population of twelve million and a capital city of the first rank, Vienna. Italy would achieve national completion, and would cease to play the rôle of the incalculable factor that she always has been in the Triple Alliance. An independent Poland, Hungary, Bohemia, and a Balkan Federation including a Roumania of ten million inhabitants on the Russian frontier, would be a mighty bulwark against Czarism. And most important of all, a democratic Germany with a population of 75,000,000 Germans could easily, without the Hohenzollerns and the ruling Junkers, come to an agreement with France and England and could isolate Czarism and condemn its foreign and internal policies to complete impotence. A policy directed towards this goal would indeed be a policy of liberation for the people of Russia as well as of Austria-Hungary. But such a policy requires an essential preliminary condition, namely, that the German people, instead of entrusting the Hohenzollerns with the liberation of other nations, should set about liberating themselves from the Hohenzollerns.

The attitude of the German and Austro-Hungarian Social Democracy in this war is in blatant contradiction to such aims. At the present moment it seems convinced of the necessity of preserving and strengthening the Hapsburg Monarchy in the interests of Germany or of the German nation. And it is absolutely from this anti-democratic viewpoint--which drives the blush of shame to the cheek of every internationally minded Socialist--that the *Wiener Arbeiter-Zeitung* formulates the historical meaning of the present War, when it declares "it is primarily a war [of the Allies] against the German spirit."

"Whether diplomacy has acted wisely, whether this has had to come, time alone can decide. Now the fate of the German nation is at stake! And there can be no hesitation, no wavering! The German people are one in the inflexible iron determination not to bend to the yoke, and neither death nor devil can succeed"--and so forth and so on. (*Wiener Arbeiter-Zeitung,* August 5th.) We will not offend the political and literary taste of the reader by continuing this quotation. Nothing is said here about the mission of liberating other nations. Here the object of the war is to preserve and secure "German humanity."

The defense of *German* culture, *German* soil, *German* humanity seems to be the mission not only of the German army but of the Austro-Hungarian army as well. Serb must fight against Serb, Pole against Pole, Ukranian against Ukranian, for the sake of *"German* humanity." The forty million non-German nationalities of Austria-Hungary are considered as simply historical manure for the field of

German culture. That this is not the standpoint of international Socialism, it is not necessary to point out. It is not even pure national democracy in its most elementary form. The Austro-Hungarian General Staff explains this "humanity" in its communiqué of September 18th: "All peoples of our revered monarchy, as our military oath says, 'against any enemy no matter whom,' must stand together as one, vying with one another in courage."

The *Wiener Arbeiter-Zeitung* accepts in its entirety this Hapsburg-Hohenzollern viewpoint of the Austro-Hungarian problem as an unnational military reservoir. It is the same attitude as the militarists of France have toward the Senegalese and the Moroccans, and the English have toward the Hindus. And when we consider that such opinions are not a new phenomenon among the German Socialists of Austria, we have found the main reason why the Austrian Social Democracy broke up so miserably into national groups, and thus reduced its political importance to a minimum.

The disintegration of the Austrian Social Democracy into national parts fighting among themselves, is one expression of the inadequacy of Austria as a state organization. At the same time the attitude of the German-Austrian Social Democracy proved that it was itself the sorry victim of this inadequacy, to which it capitulated spiritually. When it proved itself impotent to unite the many-raced Austrian proletariat under the principles of Internationalism, and finally gave up this task altogether, the Austro-German Social Democracy subordinated all Austria-Hungary and even its own policies to the "Idea" of Prussian Junker Nationalism. This utter denial of principles speaks to us in an unprecedented manner from the pages of the *Wiener Arbeiter-Zeitung*. But if we listen more carefully to the tones of this hysterical nationalism we cannot fail to hear a graver voice, the voice of history telling us that the path of political progress for Central and Southeastern Europe leads over the ruins of the Austro-Hungarian Monarchy.

CHAPTER III

THE WAR AGAINST CZARISM

But how about Czarism? Would not Germany's and Austria's victory mean the defeat of Czarism? And would not the beneficent results of the defeat of Czarism greatly outbalance the beneficent results of a dismembered Austria-Hungary?

The German and Austrian Social Democrats lay much stress upon this question in the arguing they do about the War. The crushing of a small neutral country, the ruin of France--all this is justified by the need to fight Czarism. Haase gives as the reason for voting the war credits the necessity of "defense against the danger of Russian despotism." Bernstein goes back to Marx and Engels and quotes old texts for his slogan, "Settling with Russia!"

Südekum, dissatisfied with the result of his Italian mission, says that what the Italians are to blame for is not understanding Czarism. And when the Social Democrats of Vienna and Budapest fall in line under the Hapsburg banner in its "holy war" against the Servians struggling for their national unity, they sacrifice their Socialistic honor to the necessity for fighting Czarism.

And the Social Democrats are not alone in this. The entire bourgeois German press has no other aims, for the moment, than the annihilation of the Russian autocracy, which oppresses the peoples of Russia and menaces the freedom of Europe.

The Imperial Chancellor denounces France and England as vassals of Russian despotism. Even the German Major-General von Morgen, assuredly a true and tried "friend of liberty and independence," calls on the Poles to rebel against the despotism of the Czar.

But for us who have gone through the school of historical materialism it would be a disgrace if we did not perceive the actual relations of the interests in spite of these phrases, these lies, this boasting, this foul vulgarity and stupidity.

No one can genuinely believe that the German reactionaries really do cherish such a hatred of Czarism, and are aiming their blows against it. On the contrary, after the War Czarism will be the same to the rulers of Germany that it was before the War--the most closely related form of government. Czarism is indispensable to the Germany of the Hohenzollerns, for two reasons. In the first place, it weakens Russia economically, culturally and militaristically, and so prevents its development as an imperialistic rival. In the second place, the existence of Czarism strengthens the Hohenzollern Monarchy and the Junker oligarchy, since if there were no Czarism, German absolutism would face Europe as the last mainstay of feudal barbarism.

German absolutism never has concealed the interest of blood relationship that it has in the maintenance of Czarism, which represents the same social form though in more shameless ways. Interests, tradition, sympathies draw the German reactionary element to the side Czarism. "Russia's sorrow is Germany's sorrow." At the same time the Hohenzollerns, behind the back of Czarism, can make a show of being the bulwark of culture "against barbarism," and can succeed in fooling their own people if not the rest of Western Europe.

"With sincere sorrow I see a friendship broken that Germany has kept faithfully," said William II. in his speech upon the declaration of war, referring neither to France nor to England, but to Russia, or rather, to the Russian dynasty, in accordance with the Hohenzollern's Russian religion, as Marx would have said.

We are told that Germany's political plan is to create, on the one hand, a basis of rapprochement with France and England by a victory over those countries, and, on the other hand, to utilize a strategic victory over France in order to crush Russian despotism.

The German Social Democrats must either have inspired William and his chancellor with this plan, or else must have ascribed this plan to William and his chancellor.

As a matter of fact, however, the political plans of the German reactionaries are of exactly the opposite character, must necessarily be of the opposite character.

For the present we will leave open the question of whether the destructive blow at France was dictated by strategic considerations, and whether "strategy" sanctioned defensive tactics on the Western front. But one thing is certain, that not to see that the policy of the Junkers required the ruin of France, is to prove that one has a reason for keeping one's eyes closed. France--France is the enemy!

Eduard Bernstein, who is sincerely trying to justify the political stand taken by the German Social Democracy, draws the following conclusions: Were Germany under a democratic rule, there would be no doubt as to how to settle accounts with Czarism. A democratic Germany would conduct a revolutionary war on the East. It would call on the nations oppressed by Russia to resist the tyrant and would give them the means wherewith to wage a powerful fight for freedom. [Quite right!] However, Germany is not a democracy, and therefore it would be a utopian dream [Exactly!] to expect any such policy with all its consequences from Germany as she is. (*Vorwärts*, August 28.) Very well then! But right here Bernstein suddenly breaks off his analysis of the actual German policy "with all its consequences." After showing up the blatant contradiction in the position of the German Social Democracy, he closes with the unexpected hope that a reactionary Germany may accomplish what none but a revolutionary Germany could accomplish. *Credo quid absurdum.*

Nevertheless, it might be said in opposition to this that while the ruling class in Germany has naturally no interest in fighting Czarism, still Russia is now Germany's enemy, and, quite independently of the will of the Hohenzollerns, the victory of Germany over Russia might result in the great weakening, if not the complete overthrow of Czarism. Long live Hindenburg, the great unconscious instrument of the Russian Revolution, we might cry along with the Chemnitz *Volksstimme*. Long live the Prussian Crown Prince--also a quite unconscious instrument. Long live the Sultan of Turkey who is now serving in the cause of the Revolution by bombarding the Russian cities around the Black Sea. Happy Russian Revolution--how quickly the ranks of her army are growing!

However, let us see if there is not something really to be said on this side of the question. Is it not possible that the defeat of Czarism might actually aid the cause of the Revolution?

As to such a *possibility*, there is nothing to be said against it. The Mikado and his Samurai were not in the least interested in freeing Russia, yet the Russo-Japanese War gave a powerful impetus to the revolutionary events that followed.

Consequently similar results may be expected from the German-Russian War.

But to place the right political estimate upon these historical possibilities we must take the following circumstances into consideration.

Those who believe that the Russo-Japanese War brought on the Revolution neither know nor understand historical events and their relations. The war merely hastened the outbreak of the Revolution; but for that very reason it also weakened it. For had the Revolution developed as a result of the organic growth of inner forces, it would have come later, but would have been far stronger and more systematic. Therefore, revolution has no real interest in war. This is the first consideration. And the second thing is, that while the Russo-Japanese War weakened Czarism, it strengthened Japanese militarism. The same considerations apply in a still higher degree to the present German-Russian War.

In the course of 1912-1914 Russia's enormous industrial development once for all pulled the country out of its state of counter-revolutionary depression.

The growth of the revolutionary movement on the foundation of the economic and political condition of the laboring masses, the growth of opposition in broad strata of the population, led to a new period of storm and stress. But in contrast to the years 1902-1905, this movement developed in a far more conscious, systematic manner, and, what is more, was based on a far broader social foundation. It needed time to mature, but it did not need the lances of the Prussian Samurai. On the contrary, the Prussian Samurai gave the Czar the opportunity of playing the rôle of defender of the Serbs, the Belgians and the French.

If we presuppose a catastrophal Russian defeat, the war *may* bring a quicker outbreak of the Revolution, but at the cost of its inner weakness. And if the Revolution should even gain the upper hand under such circumstances, then the bayonets of the Hohenzollern armies would be turned on the Revolution. Such a prospect can hardly fail to paralyze Russia's revolutionary forces; for it is impossible to deny the fact that the party of the German proletariat stands behind the Hohenzollern bayonets. But this is only one side of the question. The defeat of

Russia necessarily presupposes decisive victories by Germany and Austria on the other battlefields, and this would mean the enforced preservation of the national-political chaos in Central and Southeastern Europe and the unlimited mastery of German militarism in all Europe.

An enforced disarmament for France, billions in indemnities, enforced tariff walls around the conquered nations, and an enforced commercial treaty with Russia, all this in conjunction would make German imperialism master of the situation for many decades.

Germany's new policy, which began with the capitulation of the party of the proletariat to nationalistic militarism, would be strengthened for years to come. The German working class would feed itself, materially and spiritually, on the crumbs from the table of victorious imperialism, while the cause of the Social Revolution would have received a mortal blow.

That in such circumstances a Russian revolution, even if temporarily successful, would be an historical miscarriage, needs no further proof.

Consequently, this present battling of the nations under the yoke of militarism laid upon them by the capitalistic classes contains within itself monstrous contrasts which neither the War itself nor the governments directing it can solve in any way to the interest of future historical development. The Social Democrats could not, and can not now, combine their aims with any of the historical possibilities of this War, that is, with either the victory of the Triple Alliance or the victory of the Entente.

The German Social Democracy was once well aware of this. The *Vorwärts* in its issue of July 28, discussing the very question of the war against Czarism, said:

> "But if it is not possible to localize the trouble, if Russia should step into the field? What should our attitude toward Czarism be then? Herein lies the great difficulty of the situation. Has not the moment come to strike a death blow at Czarism? If German troops cross the Russian frontier, will that not mean the victory of the Russian Revolution?"

And the *Vorwärts* comes to the following conclusion:

> "Are we so sure that it *will* mean victory to the Russian Revolution if German troops cross the Russian frontier? It may readily bring the collapse of Czarism, but will not the German armies fight a revolutionary Russia with even greater energy, with a keener desire for victory, than they do the absolutistic Russia?"

More than this. On August 3, on the eve of the historical session of the Reichstag, the *Vorwärts* wrote in an article entitled "The War upon Czarism":

> "While the conservative press is accusing the strongest party in the Empire of high treason, to the rejoicing of other countries, there are other elements endeavoring to prove to the Social Democracy that the impending war is really an old Social Democratic demand. War against Russia, war upon the blood-stained and

faithless Czarism--this last is a recent phrase of the press which once kissed the knout--isn't this what Social Democracy has been asking for from the beginning? ...

"These are literally the arguments used by one portion of the bourgeois press, in fact the more intelligent portion, and it only goes to show what importance is attached to the opinion of that part of the German people which stands behind the Social Democracy. The slogan no longer is 'Russia's sorrow is Germany's sorrow.' Now it is 'Down with Czarism!' But since the days when the leaders of the Social Democracy referred to [Bebel, Lassalle, Engels, Marx] demanded a democratic war against Russia, Russia has quite ceased to be the mere palladium of reaction. Russia is also the seat of revolution. The overthrow of Czarism is now the task of all the Russian people, especially the Russian proletariat, and it is just the last weeks that have shown how vigorously this very working class in Russia is attacking the task that history has laid upon it.... And all the nationalistic attempts of the 'True Russians' to turn the hatred of the masses away from Czarism and arouse a reactionary hatred against foreign countries, particularly Germany, have failed so far. The Russian proletariat knows too well that its enemy is not beyond the border but within its own land. Nothing was more distasteful to these nationalistic agitators, the True Russians and Pan-Slavists, than the news of the great peace demonstration of the German Social Democracy. Oh, how they would have rejoiced had the contrary been the case, had they been able to say to the Russian proletariat, 'There, you see, the German Social Democrats stand at the head of those who are inciting the war against Russia!' And the Little Father in St. Petersburg would also have breathed a sigh of relief and said, 'That is the news I wanted to hear. Now the backbone of my most dangerous enemy, the Russian Revolution, is broken. The international solidarity of the proletariat is torn. Now I can unchain the beast of nationalism. I am saved!'"

Thus wrote the *Vorwärts* after Germany had already declared war on Russia.

These words characterize the honest manly stand of the proletariat against a belligerent jingoism. The *Vorwärts* clearly understood and cleverly stigmatized the base hypocrisy of the knout-loving ruling class of Germany, which suddenly became conscious of its mission to free Russia from Czarism. The *Vorwärts* warned the German working class of the political extortion that the bourgeois press would practise on their revolutionary conscience. "Do not believe these friends of the knout," the *Vorwärts* said to the German proletariat. "They are hungry for your souls, and hide their imperialistic designs behind liberal-sounding phrases. They are deceiving you--you, the cannon-fodder with souls that they need. If they succeed in winning you over, they will only be helping Czarism by dealing the Russian Revolution a fearful moral blow. And if, in spite of this, the Russian Revolu tion should raise its head, these very people will help Czarism to crush it."

That is the sense of what the *Vorwärts* preached to the working class up to the 4th of August.

And exactly three weeks later the same *Vorwärts* wrote:

> "Liberation from Muscovitism (?), freedom and independence for Poland and Finland, free development for the great Russian people themselves, dissolution of the unnatural alliance between two cultural nations and Czaristic barbarism--these were the aims that inspired the German people and made them ready for any sacrifice,"

and inspired also the German Social Democracy and its chief organ.

What happened in those three weeks to cause the *Vorwärts* to repudiate its original standpoint?

What happened? Nothing of importance. The German armies strangled neutral Belgium, burned down a number of Belgian towns, destroyed Louvain, the inhabitants of which had been so criminally audacious as to fire at the armed invaders when they themselves wore no helmets and waving feathers.[3] In those three weeks the German armies carried death and destruction into French territory, and the troops of their ally, Austria-Hungary, pounded the love of the Hapsburg Monarchy into the Serbs on the Save and the Drina. These are the facts that apparently convinced the *Vorwärts* that the Hohenzollerns were waging the war of liberation of the nations.

Neutral Belgium was crushed, and the Social Democrats remained silent. And Richard Fischer was sent to Switzerland as special envoy of the Party to explain to the people of a neutral country that the violation of Belgian neutrality and the ruin of a small nation were a perfectly natural phenomenon. Why so much excitement? Any other European government, in Germany's place, would have acted in the same way. It was just at this time that the German Social Democracy not only reconciled itself to the War as a work of real or supposed national defense, but even surrounded the Hohenzollern-Hapsburg armies with the halo of an offensive campaign for freedom. What an unprecedented fall for a party that for fifty years had taught the German working class to look upon the German Government as the foe of liberty and democracy!

In the meantime every day of the War discloses the danger to Europe that the Marxists should have foreseen at once. The chief blows of the German government were not aimed at the East, but at the West, at Belgium, France and England. Even if we accept the improbable premise that nothing but strategic necessity determined this plan of campaign, the logical political outcome of this strategy remains with all its consequences, that is, the necessity for a full and definite defeat of Belgium, France and the English land forces, so that Germany's hands might be free to deal with Russia. Wasn't it perfectly clear that what was at first represented

---

[3] "How characteristically Prussian," wrote Marx to Engels, "to declare that no man may defend his 'fatherland' except in uniform!"

as a temporary measure of strategic necessity in order to soothe the German Social Democracy, would become an end in itself through the force of events? The more stubborn the resistance made by France, whose duty it has actually become to defend its territory and its independence against the German attack, the more certainly will the German armies be held on the Western front; and the more exhausted Germany is on the Western front, the less strength and inclination will remain for her supposedly main task, the task with which the Social Democracy credited her, the "settling with Russia." And then history will witness an "honorable" peace between the two most reactionary powers of Europe, between Nicholas, to whom fate granted cheap victories over the Hapsburg Monarchy,[4] rotten to its core, and William, who had his "settling," but with Belgium, not with Russia.

The alliance between Hohenzollern and Romanoff--after the exhaustion and degradation of the Western nations--will mean a period of the darkest reaction in Europe and the whole world.

The German Social Democracy by its present policy smooths the way for this awful danger. And the danger will become an actuality unless the European proletariat interferes and enters as a revolutionary factor into the plans of the dynasties and the capitalistic governments.

---

[4] "Russian diplomacy is interested only in such wars," wrote Engels in 1890, "as force her allies to bear the chief burden of raising troops and suffering invasion, and leave to the Russian troops only the work of reserves. Czarism makes war on its own account only on decidedly weaker nations, such as Sweden, Turkey and Persia." Austria-Hungary must now be placed in the same class as Turkey and Persia.

CHAPTER IV
THE WAR AGAINST THE WEST

On his return from his diplomatic trip to Italy, Dr. Südekum wrote in the *Vorwärts* that the Italian comrades did not sufficiently comprehend the nature of Czarism. We agree with Dr. Südekum that a German can more easily understand the nature of Czarism as he experiences daily, in his own person, the nature of Prussian-German absolutism. The two "natures" are very closely akin to each other.

German absolutism represents a feudal-monarchical organization, resting upon a mighty capitalist foundation, which the development of the last half-century has erected for it. The strength of the German army, as we have learned to know it anew in its present bloody work, consists not alone in the great material and technical resources of the nation, and in the intelligence and precision of the workman-soldier, who had been drilled in the school of industry and his own class organizations. It has its foundation also in its Junker officer caste, with its master class traditions, its oppression of those who are below and its subordination to those who are above. The German army, like the German state, is a feudal-monarchical organization with inexhaustible capitalistic resources. The bourgeois scribblers may chatter all they want about the supremacy of the German, the man of duty, over the Frenchman, the man of pleasure; the real difference lies not in the racial qualities, but in the social and political conditions. The standing army, that closed corporation, that self-sufficing state within the state, remains, despite universal military service, a caste organization that in order to thrive must have artificial distinctions of rank and a monarchical top to crown the commanding hierarchy.

In his work, "The New Army," Jaurès showed that the only army France could have is an army of defense built on the plan of arming every citizen, that is, a democratic army, a *militia*. The bourgeois French Republic is now paying the penalty for having made her army a counterpoise to her democratic state organization. She created, in Jaurès' words, "a bastard régime in which antiquated forms clashed with newly developing forms and neutralized each other." This incongruity between the standing army and the republican régime is the fundamental weakness of the French military system.

The reverse is true of Germany. Germany's barbarian retrograde political system gives her a great military supremacy. The German bourgeoisie may grumble now and then when the pretorian caste spirit of the officers' corps leads to outbreaks like that of Zabern. They may make wry faces at the Crown Prince and his slogan, "Give it to them! Give it to them!" The German Social Democracy may inveigh ever so sharply against the systematic personal ill-treatment of the German soldier which has caused proportionately double the number of suicides in the German barracks of that in any other country. But for all that, the fact that the German bourgeoisie has absolutely no political character and that the German Socialist party has failed to inspire the proletariat with the revolutionary spirit has enabled the ruling class to erect the gigantic structure of militarism, and so place the efficient and intelligent German workmen under the command of the Zabern heroes and their slogan, "Give it to them!"

Professor Hans Delbrück seeks the source of Germany's military strength in the ancient model of the Teutoburgerwald, and he is perfectly justified.

> "The oldest Germanic system of warfare," he writes, "was based on the retinue of princes, a body of specially selected warriors, and the mass of fighters comprising the entire nation. This is the system we have to-day also. How vastly different are the methods of fighting now from those of our ancestors in the Teutoburgerwald! We have the technical marvels of modern machine guns. We have the wonderful organization of immense masses of troops. And yet, our military system is at bottom the same. The martial spirit is raised to its highest power, developed to its utmost in a body which once was small but now numbers many thousands, a body giving fealty to their War Lord, and by him, as by the princes of old, regarded as his comrades; and under their leadership the whole people, educated by them and disciplined by them. *Here we have the secret of the warlike character of the German nation.*"

The French Major, Driant, looks on at the German Kaiser in his White Cuirassier's uniform, undoubtedly the most imposing military uniform in the world, and republican by constraint that he is, his heart is filled with a lover's jealousy. And how the Kaiser spends his time "in the midst of his army, that true family of the Hohenzollerns!" The Major is fascinated.

The feudal caste, whose hour of political and moral decay had struck long ago, found its connection with the nation once more in the fertile soil of imperialism. And this connection with the nation has taken such deep root that the prophecies of Major Driant, written several years ago, have actually come true--prophecies that until now could only have appeared as either the poisonous promptings of a secret Bonapartist, or the drivellings of a lunatic.

> "The Kaiser," he wrote, "is the Commander in Chief ... and behind him stands the entire working class of Germany as one man.... Bebel's Social Democrats are in the ranks, their fingers on the trigger, and they too think only of the welfare of the Fatherland. The ten-billion war indemnity that France will have to pay will be a greater help to them than the Socialist chimeras on which they fed the day before."

Yes, and now they are writing of this future indemnity even in some *Social Democratic (!)* papers, with open rowdy insolence--an indemnity, however, not of ten billions, but of twenty or thirty billions.

Germany's victory over France--a deplorable strategic necessity, according to the German Social Democrats--would mean not only the defeat of France's standing army; it would mean primarily the victory of the feudal-monarchical state over the democratic-republican state.

For the ancient race of Hindenburgs, Moltkes and Klucks, hereditary specialists in mass-murder, are just as indispensable a condition of German victory as are the 42 centimeter guns, the last word in human technical skill.

The entire capitalist press is already talking of the unshakable stability of the German Monarchy, strengthened by the war. And German professors, the same who proclaimed Hindenburg a doctor of All the Sciences, are already declaring that political slavery is a higher form of social life.

> "The democratic republics, and the so-called monarchies that are under subjection to a parliamentary régime, and all the other beautiful things that were so extolled--what little capacity they have shown to stand the storm!"

These are the things that the German professors are writing now.

It is shameful and humiliating enough to read the expressions of the French Socialists, who had proved themselves too weak to break the alliance of France with Russia or even to prevent the return to three-years' military service, but who, when the War began, nevertheless donned their red trousers and set out to free Germany. But we are seized with a feeling of unspeakable indignation on reading the German Socialist party press, which in the language of exalted slaves extols the brave heroic caste of hereditary oppressors for their armed exploits on French territory.

On August 15, 1870, when the victorious German armies were approaching Paris, Engels wrote in a letter to Marx, after describing the confused condition of the French defense:

> "Nevertheless, a revolutionary government, if it comes soon, need not despair. But it must leave Paris to its fate, and continue to carry on the war from the south. It is then still possible that such a government may hold out until arms and ammunition are bought and a new army organized with which the enemy can be gradually pushed back to the frontier. That would be the right ending to the war--for both countries to demonstrate that they cannot be conquered."

And yet there are people who shout like drunken helots, "On to Paris." And in doing so they have the impudence to invoke the names of Marx and Engels. In what measure are they superior to the thrice despised Russian liberals who crawled on their bellies before his Excellency, the military Commander, who introduced the Russian knout into East Galicia. It is cowardly arrogance--this talk of the purely "strategic" character of the War on the Western front. Who takes any account of it? Certainly not the German ruling classes. They speak the language of conviction and of main force. They call things by their right names. They know what they want and they know how to fight for it.

The Social Democrats tell us that the War is being waged for the cause of national independence. "That is not true," retorted Herr Arthur Dix.

> "Just as the high politics of the last century," wrote Dix, "owed its specially marked character to the *National Idea*, so the political-world events of this century stand under the emblem of the *Imperialistic Idea*. The imperialistic idea that is destined to give the impetus, the scope and the goal to the striving for power of the great (*Der Weltwirtschaftskrieg*, 1914, p. 3).

> "It shows gratifying sagacity," says the same Herr Arthur Dix, "on the part of those who had charge of the military preparations of the War, that the advance of our armies against France and Russia in the very first stage of the War took place precisely where it was most important to keep valuable German mineral wealth free from foreign invasion, and to occupy such portions of the enemy's territory as would supplement our own underground resources" (Ibid., p. 38).

The "strategy," of which the Socialists now speak in devout whispers, really begins its activities with the robbery of mineral wealth.

The Social Democrats tell us that the War is a war of defense. But Herr Georg Irmer says clearly and distinctly:

> "People ought not to be talking as though the German nation had come too late for rivalry for world economy and world dominion,--that the world has already been divided. Has not the earth been divided over and over again in all epochs of history?" (*Los vom englischen Weltjoch*, 1914, p. 42.)

The Socialists try to comfort us by telling us that Belgium has only been temporarily crushed and that the Germans will soon vacate their Belgian quarters. But Herr Arthur Dix, who knows very well what he wants, and who has the right and the power to want it, writes that what England fears most, and expressly so, is that *Germany should have an outlet to the Atlantic Ocean.*

"For this very reason," he continues, "we must neither *let Belgium go out of our hands*, nor must we fail to make sure that the coast line from Ostende to the Somme shall not again fall into the hands of any state which may become a political vassal of England. We must see to it that in some form or other *German influence* is securely established there."

In the endless battles between Ostende and Dunkirk, sacred "strategy" is now carrying out this programme of the Berlin stock exchange, also.

The Socialists tell us that the War between France and Germany is merely a brief prelude to a lasting alliance between those countries. But here, too, Herr

Arthur Dix shows Germany's cards. According to him, "there is but one answer: *to seek to destroy the English world trade, and to deal deadly blows at English national economy.*"

"The aim for the foreign policy of the German Empire for the next decades is clearly indicated," Professor Franz von Liszt announces. "'Protection against England,' that must be our slogan" (*Ein mitteleuropäischer Staatenverband,* 1914, p. 24).

> "We must crush the most treacherous and malicious of our foes," cries a third. "We must break the tyranny which England exercises over the sea with base self-seeking and shameless contempt of justice and right."

The War is directed not against Czarism, but primarily against England's supremacy on the sea.

> "It may be said," Professor Schiehmann confesses, "that no success of ours has given us such joy as the defeat of the English at Maubeuge and St. Quentin on August 28."

The German Social Democrats tell us that the chief object of the War is the "settlement with Russia." But plain, straightforward Herr Rudolf Theuden wants to give Galicia to Russia with North Persia thrown in. Then Russia "would have got enough to be satisfied for many decades to come. We may even make her our friend by it."

"What ought the War to bring us?" asks Theuden, and then he answers:

> "*The chief payment must be made us by France....* France must give us Belfort, that part of Lorraine which borders on the Moselle, and, in case of stubborn resistance, that part as well which borders on the Maas. If we make the Maas and the Moselle German boundaries, the French will some day perhaps wean themselves away from the idea of making the Rhine a French boundary."

The bourgeois politicians and professors tell us that England is the chief enemy; that Belgium and France are the gateway to the Atlantic Ocean; that the hope of a Russian indemnity is only a Utopian dream, anyway; that Russia would be more useful as friend than as foe; that France will have to pay in land and in gold--and the *Vorwärts* exhorts the German workers to "hold out until the decisive victory is ours."

And yet the *Vorwärts* tells us that the War is being waged for the independence of the German nation, and for the liberation of the Russian people. What does this mean? Of course we must not look for ideas, logic and truth where they do not exist. This is simply a case of an ulcer of slavish sentiments bursting open and foul pus crawling over the pages of the workingmen's press. It is clear that the oppressed class which proceeds too slowly and inertly on its way toward freedom must in the final hour drag all its hopes and promises through mire and blood, before there arises in its soul the pure, unimpeachable voice--the voice of revolutionary honor.

CHAPTER V

THE WAR OF DEFENSE

"The thing for us to do now is to avert this danger [Russian despotism], and to secure the culture and the independence of our land. Thus we will make good our word, and do what we have always said we would. In the hour of danger we will not leave our Fatherland in the lurch.... Guided by these principles we vote for the war credits."

This was the declaration of the German Social Democratic fraction, read by Haase in the Reichstag session of August 4.

Here only the defense of the fatherland is mentioned. Not a word is said of the "liberating" mission of this War in behalf of the peoples of Russia, which was later sung in every key by the Social Democratic press. The logic of the Socialist press, however, did not keep pace with its patriotism. For while it made desperate efforts to represent the War as one of pure defense, to secure the safety of Germany's possessions, it at the same time pictured it as a revolutionary offensive war for the liberation of Russia and of Europe from Czarism.

We have already shown clearly enough why the peoples of Russia had every reason to decline with thanks the assistance offered them at the point of the Hohenzollern bayonets. But how about the "defensive" character of the War?

What surprises us even more than what is said in the declaration of the Social Democracy is what it conceals and leaves unsaid. After Hollweg had already announced in the Reichstag the accomplished violation of the neutrality of Belgium and Luxemburg as a means of attacking France, Haase does not mention this fact in a single word. This silence is so monstrous that one is tempted to read the declaration a second and a third time. But in vain. The declaration is written as though such countries as Belgium, France and England had never existed on the political map of the German Social Democracy.

But facts do not cease to be facts simply because political parties shut their eyes to them. And every member of the International has the right to ask this question of Comrade Haase, "What portion of the five billions voted by the Social Democratic fraction was meant for the destruction of Belgium?" It is quite possible that in order to protect the German fatherland from Russian despotism it was inevitable that the Belgian fatherland should be crushed. But why did the Social Democratic fraction keep silent on this point?

The reason is clear. The English Liberal government, in its effort to make the War popular with the masses, made its plea exclusively on the ground of the necessity of protecting the independence of Belgium and the integrity of France, but utterly ignored its alliance with Russian Czarism. In like manner, and from the same motives, the German Social Democracy speaks to the masses only about the war against Czarism, but does not mention even by name Belgium, France and England. All this is of course not exactly flattering to the international reputation of Czarism. Yet it is quite distressing that the German Social Democracy should sacrifice its own good name to the call to arms against Czarism. Lassalle said that every great political action should begin with a statement of things as they are. Then why does the defense of the Fatherland begin with an abashed silence as to things as they are? Or did the German Social Democracy perhaps think that this was not a "big political action"?

Anyway, the defense of the Fatherland is a very broad and very elastic conception. The world catastrophe began with Austria's ultimatum to Serbia. Austria, naturally, was guided solely by the need of defending her borders from her uneasy neighbor. Austria's prop was Germany. And Germany, in turn, as we already know, was prompted by the need to secure her own state. "It would be senseless to believe," writes Ludwig Quessel on this point, "that one wall could be torn away from this extremely complex structure (Europe) without endangering the security of the whole edifice."

Germany opened her "Defensive War" with an attack upon Belgium, the violation of Belgium's neutrality being allegedly only a means of breaking through to France along the line of least resistance. The military defeat of France also was to appear only as a strategic episode in the defense of the Fatherland.

To some German patriots this construction of things did not seem quite plausible, and they had good grounds for disbelieving it. They suspected a motive which squared far better with the reality. Russia, entering upon a new era of military preparation, would be a far greater menace to Germany in two or three years than she was then. And France during that time would have completely carried out her three-year army reform. Is it not clear, then, that an intelligent self-defense demanded that Germany should not wait for the attack of her enemies but should anticipate them by two years and take the offensive at once? And isn't it clear, too, that such an offensive war, deliberately provoked by Germany and Austria, is in reality a preventive war of defense?

Not infrequently these two points of view are combined in a single argument. Granted that there is some slight contradiction between them. The one declares that Germany did not want the War now and that it was forced upon her by the Triple Entente, while the other implies that war was disadvantageous to the Entente now and that for that very reason Germany had taken the initiative to bring on the War at this time. But what if there is this contradiction? It is lightly and easily glossed over and reconciled in the saving concept of a war of defense.

But the belligerents on the other side disputed this advantageous position of being on the defensive, which Germany sought to assume, and did it successfully.

France could not permit the defeat of Russia on the ground of her own self-defense. England gave as the motive for her interference the immediate danger to the British Islands which a strengthening of Germany's position at the mouth of the Channel would mean. Finally, Russia, too, spoke only of self-defense. It is true that no one threatened Russian territory. But national possessions, mark you, do not consist merely in territory, but in other, intangible, factors as well, among them, the influence over weaker states. Servia "belongs" in the sphere of Russian influence and serves the purpose of maintaining the so-called balance of power in the Balkans, not only the balance of power between the Balkan States but also between Russian and Austrian influence. A successful Austrian attack on Servia threatened to disturb this balance of power in Austria's favor, and therefore meant an indirect attack upon Russia. Sasonov undoubtedly found his strongest argument in Quessel's words: "It would be senseless to believe that one wall could be torn away from the extremely complex structure (Europe) without endangering the security of the entire edifice."

It is superfluous to add that Servia and Montenegro, Belgium and Luxemburg, could also produce some proofs of the defensive character of their policies. Thus, all the countries were on the defensive, none was the aggressor. But if that is so, then what sense is there in opposing the claims of defensive and offensive war to each other? The standards applied in such cases differ greatly, and are not frequently quite incommensurable.

What is of fundamental importance to us Socialists is the question of the *historical* rôle of the War. Is the War calculated to effectively promote the productive forces and the state organizations, and to accelerate the concentration of the working class forces? Or is the reverse true, will it hinder in this? This materialistic evaluation of wars stands above all formal or external considerations, and in its nature has no relation to the question of defense or aggression. And yet sometimes these formal expressions about a war designate with more or less truth the actual significance of the war. When Engels said that the Germans were on the defensive in 1870, he had least of all the immediate political and diplomatic circumstances in mind. The determining fact for him was that in that war Germany was fighting for her right to national unity, which was a necessary condition for the economic development of the country and the Socialist consolidation of the proletariat. In the same sense the Christian peoples of the Balkans waged a war of defense against Turkey, fighting for their right to independent national development against the foreign rule.

The question of the immediate international political conditions leading to a war is independent of the value the war possesses from the *historico-materialistic* point of view. The German war against the Bonapartist Monarchy was historically unavoidable. In that war the right of development was on the German side. Yet those historical tendencies did not, in themselves, predetermine the question as to which party was interested in provoking the war just in the year 1870. We know now very well that international politics and military considerations induced Bismarck to take the actual initiative in the war. It might have happened just the other way, however. With greater foresight and energy, the government of Napoleon III could have anticipated Bismarck, and begun the war a few years earlier. That would have radically changed the immediate political aspect of events, but it would have made no difference in the historic estimate of the war.

Third in order is the factor of diplomacy. Diplomacy here has a two-fold task to perform. First, it must bring about war at the moment most favorable for its own country from the international as well as the military standpoint. Second, it must employ methods which throw the burden of responsibility for the bloody conflict, in public opinion, on the enemy government. The exposure of diplomatic trickery, cheating and knavery is one of the most important functions of Socialist political agitation. But no matter to what extent we succeed in this at the crucial juncture, it is clear that the net of diplomatic intrigues in themselves signifies nothing either as regards the historic rôle of the war or its real initiators. Bismarck's clever manoeuvres forced Napoleon III to declare war on Prussia, although the actual initiative came from the German side.

Next follows the purely military aspect. The *strategic* plan of operations can be calculated chiefly for defense or attack, regardless of which side declared the war and under what conditions. Finally, the first tactics followed in the carrying out of the strategic plan not infrequently plays a great part in estimating the war as a war of defense or of aggression.

> "It is a good thing," wrote Engels to Marx on July 31, 1870, "that the French attacked first on German soil. If the Germans repel the invasion and follow it up by invading French territory, then it will certainly not produce the same impression as if the Germans had marched into France without a previous invasion. In this way the war remains, on the French side, more Bonapartistic."

Thus we see by the classic example of the Franco-Prussian War that the standards for judging whether a war is defensive or aggressive are full of contradictions when two nations clash. Then how much more so are they when it is a clash of several nations. If we unroll the tangle from the beginning, we arrive at the following connection between the elements of attack and defense. The first *tactical* move of the French should--at least in Engels' opinion--make the people feel that the responsibility of attack rested with the French. And yet the entire *strategic* plan of the Germans had an absolutely aggressive character. The *diplomatic* moves of Bismarck forced Bonaparte to declare war against his will and thus appear as the disturber of the peace of Europe, while the military-political initiative in the war came from the Prussian government. These circumstances are by no means of slight importance for the *historical* estimate of the war, but they are not at all exhaustive.

One of the causes of this war was the growing ambition of the Germans for national self-determination, which conflicted with the dynastic pretensions of the French Monarchy. But this national "war of defense" led to the annexation of Alsace-Lorraine and so in its second stage turned into a dynastic war of conquest.

The correspondence between Marx and Engels shows that they were guided chiefly by historical considerations in their attitude towards the War of 1870. To them, of course, it was by no means a matter of indifference as to who conducted the war and how it was conducted. "Who would have thought it possible," Marx writes bitterly, "that twenty-two years after 1848 a nationalist war in Germany could have been given such theoretical expression." Yet what was of decisive significance to Marx and Engels was the objective consequences of the war. "If the Prussians triumph, it will mean the centralization of the state power--useful to the centralization of the German working-class."

Liebknecht and Bebel, starting with the same historical estimate of the war, were directly forced to take a political position toward it. It was by no means in opposition to the views of Marx and Engels, but, on the contrary, with their perfect acquiescence that Liebknecht and Bebel refused, in the Reichstag, to take any responsibility for this War. The statement they handed in read:

> "We cannot grant the war appropriations that the Reichstag is asked to make because that would be a vote of confidence in the Prussian government.... As opponents on principle of every dynastic war, as Social Republicians and members of the International Labor Association, which, without distinction of nationality, fights all oppressors and endeavors to unite all the oppressed in one great brotherhood, we cannot declare ourselves either directly or indirectly in favor of the present war."

Schweitzer acted differently. He took the historical estimate of the war as a direct guide for his tactics--one of the most dangerous of fallacies!--and in voting the war credits gave a vote of confidence to the policy of Bismarck. And this in spite of the fact that it was necessary, if the centralization of state power arising out of the War was to turn out of use to the Social Democratic cause, that the working-class should from the very beginning oppose the dynastic-Junker centralization with their own class-centralization filled with revolutionary distrust of the rulers.

Schweitzer's political attitude invalidated the very consequences of the War that had induced him to give a vote of confidence to the makers of the War.

Forty years later, drawing up the balance sheet of his life-work, Bebel wrote:

> "The attitude that Liebknecht and I took at the outbreak and during the continuance of the war has for years been a subject of discussion and violent attack, at first even in the Party; but only for a short time. Then they acknowledged that we had been right. I confess that I do not in any way regret our attitude, and if at the outbreak of the War we had known what we learned within the next few years from the official and unofficial disclosures, our attitude from the very start would have been still harsher. We would not merely have abstained, as we did, from voting the first war credits, we would have voted *against* them." (*Autobiography*, Part II, p. 167.)

If we compare the Liebknecht-Bebel statement of 1870 with Haase's declaration in 1914, we must conclude that Bebel was mistaken when he said, "Then they acknowledged that we had been right." For the vote of August 4 was eminently a condemnation of Bebel's policy forty-four years earlier, since in Haase's phraseology, Bebel had then left the Fatherland in the lurch in the hour of danger.

What political causes and considerations have led the party of the German proletariat to abandon its glorious traditions? Not a single weighty reason has been given so far. All the arguments adduced are full of contradictions. They are like diplomatic communiqués which are written to justify an already accomplished act. The leader writer of *Die Neue Zeit* writes--with the blessing of Comrade Kautsky--that Germany's position towards Czarism is the same as it was towards Bonapartism in 1870! He even quotes from a letter of Engels: "All classes of the German people realized that it was a question, first of all, of national existence, and so they fell in line at once." For the same reason, we are told, the German Social Democracy has fallen into line now. It is a question of national existence. "Substitute Czarism for Bonapartism, and Engels' words are true to-day." And yet the fact remains, in all its force, that Bebel and Liebknecht demonstratively refused to vote either money or confidence to the government in 1870. Does it not hold just as well, then, if we "substitute Czarism for Bonapartism"? To this question no answer has been vouchsafed.

But what did Engels really write in his letter concerning the tactics of the labor party?

"It does not seem possible to me that under such circumstances a German political party can preach *total obstruction*, and place all sorts of minor considerations above the main issue." *Total obstruction!*--But there is a wide gap between total obstruction and the total capitulation of a political party. And it was this gap that divided the positions between Bebel and Schweitzer in 1870. Marx and Engels were with Bebel against Schweitzer. Comrade Kautsky might have informed his leader writer, Hermann Wendel, of this fact. And it is nothing but defamation of the dead for *Simplicissimus* now to reconcile the shades of Bebel and Bismarck in Heaven. If *Simplicissimus* and Wendel have the right to awaken anybody from his sleep in the grave for the endorsement of the present tactics of the German Social Democracy, then it is not Bebel, but Schweitzer. It is the shade of Schweitzer that now oppresses the political party of the German proletariat.

But the very analogy between the Franco-Prussian War and the present War is superficial and misleading in the extreme. Let us set aside all the international relations. Let us forget that the War meant first of all the destruction of Belgium, and that Germany's main force was hurled not against Czarism but republican France. Let us forget that the starting point of the War was the crushing of Servia, and that one of its aims was the strengthening and consolidation of the arch-reactionary state, Austria-Hungary. We will not dwell on the fact that the attitude of the German Social Democracy dealt a hard blow at the Russian Revolution, which in the two years before the War had again flared up in such a tempest. We will close our eyes to all these facts, just as the German Social Democracy did on August 4th, when it did not see that there was a Belgium in the world, a France, England, Servia, or Austria-Hungary. We will grant only the existence of Germany.

In 1870 it was quite easy to estimate the historical significance of the war. "If the Prussians win, the centralization of state power will further the centralization of the German working class." And now? What would be the result for the German working class of a Prussian victory now?

The only territorial expansion which the German working class could welcome, because it would complete the national unity, is a union of German Austria with Germany. Any other expansion of the German fatherland means another step towards the transformation of Germany from a national state to a state of nationalities, and the consequent introduction of all those conditions which render more difficult the class struggle of the proletariat.

Ludwig Frank hoped--and he expressed this hope in the language of a belated Lassallian--that later, after a victorious war, he would devote himself to the work of the "internal building up" of the state. There is no doubt that Germany will need this "internal building up" after a victory no less than before the War. But will a victory make this work easier? There is nothing in Germany's historical experiences any more than in those of any other country to justify such a hope.

> "We regarded the doings of the rulers of Germany [after the victories of 1870] as a matter of course," says Bebel in his *Autobiography*. "It was merely an illusion of the Party Executive to believe that a more liberal spirit would prevail in the new order. And this more liberal régime was to be granted by the same man who had till then shown himself the greatest enemy, I will not say of democratic development, but even of every liberal tendency, and who now as victor planted the heel of his Cuirassier boot on the neck of the new Empire." (Vol. II, p. 188.)

There is absolutely no reason to expect different results now from a victory from above. On the contrary. In 1870 Prussian Junkerdom had first to adapt itself to the new imperial order. It could not feel secure in the saddle all at once. It was eight years after the victory over France that the anti-Socialist laws were passed. In forty-four years Prussian Junkerdom has become the imperial Junkerdom. And if, after half a century of the most intense class struggle, Junkerdom should appear at the head of the victorious nation, then we need not doubt that it would not have felt the need of Ludwig Frank's services for the internal building up of the state had he returned safe from the fields of German victories.

But far more important than the strengthening of the class position of the rulers is the influence a German victory would have upon the proletariat itself. The war grew out of imperialistic antagonisms between the capitalist states, and the victory of Germany, as stated above, can produce only one result--territorial acquisitions at the expense of Belgium, France and Russia, commercial treaties forced upon her enemies, and new colonies. The class struggle of the proletariat would then be placed upon the basis of the imperialistic hegemony of Germany, the working class would be interested in the maintenance and development of this hegemony, and revolutionary Socialism would for a long time be condemned to the rôle of a propagandist sect.

Marx was right when in 1870 he foresaw, as a result of the German victories, a rapid development for the German labor movement under the banner of scientific Socialism. But now the international conditions point to the very opposite prognosis. Germany's victory would mean the taking of the edge off the revolutionary movement, its theoretic shallowing, and the dying out of the Marxist ideas.

CHAPTER VI

WHAT HAVE SOCIALISTS TO DO
WITH CAPITALIST WARS?

But the German Social Democracy, we shall be told, does not want victory. Our answer must be in the first place that this is not true. What the German Social Democracy wants is told by its press. With two or three exceptions Socialist papers daily point out to the German workingman that a victory of the German arms is *his* victory. The capture of Maubeuge, the sinking of three English warships, or the fall of Antwerp aroused in the Social Democratic press the same feelings that otherwise are excited by the gain of a new election district or a victory in a wage dispute. We must not lose sight of the fact that the German labor press, the Party press as well as the trade union papers, is now a powerful mechanism that in place of the education of the people's will for the class struggle has substituted the education of the people's will for military victories. I have not in mind the ugly chauvinistic excesses of individual organs, but the underlying sentiment of the overwhelming majority of the Social Democratic papers. The signal for this attitude seems to have been given by the vote of the fraction on August 4th.

But the fraction wasn't thinking of a German victory. It made it its task only to avert the danger threatening from the outside, to defend the Fatherland. That was all.

And here we come back to the question of wars of defense and wars of aggression. The German press, including the Social Democratic organs, does not cease to repeat that it is Germany of all countries that finds itself on the defensive in this War. We have already discussed the standards for determining the difference between a war of aggression and a war of defense. These standards are numerous and contradictory. Yet in the present case they testify unanimously that Germany's military acts cannot possibly be construed as the acts of a war of defense. But this has absolutely no influence upon the tactics of the Social Democracy.

From a *historical* standpoint the new German imperialism is, as we already know, absolutely aggressive. Urged onward by the feverish development of the national industry, German imperialism disturbs the old balance of power between the states and plays the first violin in the race for armaments.

And from the *standpoint of world politics* the present moment seemed to be most favorable for Germany to deal her rivals a crushing blow--which however does not lessen the guilt of Germany's enemies by one iota.

The *diplomatic* view of events leaves no doubt concerning the leading part that Germany played in Austria's provocative action in Servia. The fact that Czarist diplomacy was, as usual, still more disgraceful, does not alter the case.

From the standpoint of *strategy* the entire German campaign was based on a monstrous offensive.

And finally from the standpoint of *tactics*, the first move of the German army was the violation of Belgian neutrality.

If all this is defense, then what is attack? But even if we assume that events as pictured in the language of diplomacy admit of other interpretations--although the first two pages of the White Book are very clear as to this meaning--has the revolutionary party of the working class no other standards for determining its policy than the documents presented by a government that has the greatest interest in deceiving it?

> "Bismarck duped the whole world," says Bebel, "and knew how to make people believe that it was Napoleon who provoked the war, while he himself, the peace-loving Bismarck, found himself and his policy in the position of being attacked.
>
> "The events preceding the war were so misleading that France's complete unpreparedness for the war that she herself declared was generally overlooked, while in Germany, which appeared to be the one attacked, preparations for war had been completed down to the very last wagon-nail, and mobilization moved with the precision of clockwork." (*Autobiography*, Vol. III, pages 167-168.)

After such an historical precedent one might expect more critical caution from the Social Democracy.

It is quite true that Bebel more than once repeated his assertion that in case of an attack on Germany the Social Democracy would defend its Fatherland. At the convention held at Essen, Kautsky answered him:

> "In my opinion we cannot promise positively to share the government's war enthusiasm every time we are convinced that the country is threatened by attack. Bebel thinks we are much further advanced than we were in 1870 and that we are now able to decide in every instance whether the war which threatens is really one of aggression or not. I should not like to take this responsibility upon myself. I should not like to undertake to guarantee that we could make a correct decision in every instance, that we shall always know whether a government is deceiving us, or whether it is not actually representing the interests of the nation against a war of attack.... Yesterday it was the German government that took the aggressive, to-morrow it will be the French government, and we cannot know if the day after it may not be the English government. The governments are constantly taking

turns. As a matter of fact what we are concerned with in case of war is not a national, but an international question. For a war between great powers will become a world war and will affect the whole of Europe, not two countries alone. Some day the German government might make the German proletariat believe they were being attacked; the French government might do the same with its subjects, and then we should have a war in which the French and German working men would follow their respective governments with equal enthusiasm, and murder each other and cut each other's throats. Such a contingency must be avoided, and it will be avoided if we do not adopt the criterion of the aggressive or defensive war, but that of the interests of the proletariat, which at the same time are international interests.... Fortunately, it is a misconception to assume that the German Social Democracy in case of war wanted to judge by national and not by international considerations, and felt itself to be first a German and then a proletariat party."

With splendid clearness Kautsky in this speech reveals the terrible dangers--now a still more terrible actuality--that are latent in the endeavor to make the position of the Social Democracy dependent upon an indefinite and contradictory formal estimate of whether a war is one of defense or one of aggression. Bebel in his reply said nothing of importance; and his point of view seemed quite inexplicable, especially after his own experiences of the year 1870.

Nevertheless, in spite of its theoretical inadequacy, Bebel's position had a quite definite political meaning. Those imperialistic tendencies which the danger of war begat excluded the possibility for the Social Democracy's expecting salvation from the victory of either of the warring parties. For that very reason its entire attention was directed to the preventing of war, and the principal task was to keep the governments worried about the results of a war.

"The Social Democracy," said Bebel, "will oppose any government which takes the initiative in war." He meant this as a threat to William II.'s government. "Don't reckon upon us if some day you decide to utilize your cannon and your battleships." Then he turned to Petrograd and London: "They had better take care not to attack Germany in a miscalculation of weakness from within on account of the obstructionist policies of the powerful German Social Democracy."

Without being a political doctrine, Bebel's conception was a political threat, and a threat directed simultaneously at two fronts, the internal front and the foreign front. His one obstinate answer to all historical and logical objections was: "We'll find the way to expose any government that takes the first step towards war. We are clever enough for that."

This threatening attitude of not only the German Social Democracy but also of the International Party was not without results. The various governments actually did make every effort to postpone the outbreak of the War. But that is not all. The rulers and the diplomats were doubly attentive now to adapting their moves to the pacifist psychology of the masses. They whispered with the Socialist leaders, nosed about in the office of the International, and so created a sentiment which made it possible for Jaurès and Haase to declare at Brussels, a few days before the outbreak of the War, that their particular governments had no other object than the preservation of peace. And when the storm broke loose, the Social Democracy of every country looked for the guilty party--on the other side of the border. Bebel's utterance, which had played a definite part as a threat, lost all meaning the instant the first shots were fired at the frontiers. That terrible thing took place which Kautsky had prophesied.

What at first glance appears the most surprising thing about it all is, that the Social Democracy had not really felt the need for a political criterion. In the catastrophe that has occurred to the International the arguments have been notable for their superficiality. They contradicted each other, shifted ground, and were of only secondary significance--the gist of the matter being that the *fatherland must be defended*. Apart from considerations of the historical outcome of the War, apart from considerations of democracy and the class struggle, the fatherland that has come down to us historically must be defended. And defended not because our government wanted peace and was "perfidiously attacked," as the international penny-a-liners put it, but because apart from the conditions or the ways in which it was provoked, apart from who was right and who was wrong, war, once it breaks out, subjects every belligerent to the danger of invasion and conquest. Theoretical, political, diplomatic and military considerations fall into ruins as in an earthquake, a conflagration or a flood. The government with its army is elevated to the position of the one power that can protect and save its people. The large masses of the people in actuality return to a pre-political condition. This feeling of the masses, this elemental reflex of the catastrophe, need not be criticized in so far as it is only a temporary feeling. But it is quite a different matter in the case of the attitude of the Social Democracy, the responsible political representative of the masses. The political organizations of the possessing classes and especially the power of the government itself did not simply float with the stream. They instantly set to work most intensively and in very varied ways to heighten this unpolitical sentiment and to unite the masses around the army and the government. The Social Democracy not only did not become equally active in the opposite direction, but from the very first moment surrendered to the policy of the government and to the elemental feeling of the masses. And instead of arming these masses with the weapons of criticism and distrust, if only passive criticism and distrust, it itself by its whole attitude hastened the people along the road to this pre-political condition. It renounced its traditions and political pledges of fifty years with a conspicuous readiness that was least of all calculated to inspire the rulers with respect.

Bethmann-Hollweg announced that the German government was in absolute agreement with the German people, and after the avowal of the *Vorwärts*, in view of the position taken by the Social Democracy, he had a perfect right to say so. But he had still another right. If conditions had not induced him to postpone political polemics to a more favorable moment, he might have said at the Reichstag session of August 4th, addressing the representatives of the Socialist proletariat: "To-day you agree with us in recognizing the danger threatening our Fatherland, and you join us in trying to avert the danger by arms. But this danger has not grown up since yesterday. You must previously have known of the existence and the tendencies of Czarism, and you knew that we had other enemies besides. So by what right did you attack us when we built up our army and our navy? By what right did you refuse to vote for military appropriations year after year? Was it by the right of treason or the right of blindness? If in spite of you we had not built up our army, we should now be helpless in the face of this Russian menace that has brought you to your senses, too. No appropriations granted now could enable us to make up for what we would have lost. We should now be without arms, without cannons, without fortifications. Your voting to-day in favor of the war credit of five billion is an admission that your annual refusal of the budget was only an empty demonstration, and, worse than that, was political demagogy. For as soon as you came up for a serious historical examination, you denied your entire past!"

That is what the German Chancellor could have said, and this time his speech would have carried conviction. And what could Haase have replied?

"We never took a stand for Germany's disarmament in the face of dangers from without. Such peace rubbish was never in our thoughts. As long as international contradictions create out of themselves the danger of war, we want Germany to be safe against foreign invasion and servitude. What we are trying for is a military organization which cannot--as can an artificially trained organization--be made to serve for class exploitation at home and for imperialistic adventures abroad, but will be invincible in national defense. We want a militia. We cannot trust you with the work of national defense. You have made the army a school of reactionary training. You have drilled your corps of officers in the hatred of the most important class of modern society, the proletariat. You are capable of risking millions of lives, not for the real interests of the people, but for the selfish interests of the ruling minority, which you veil with the names of national ideals and state prestige. We do not trust you, and that is why we have declared year after year, 'Not a single man or a single penny for this class government!"

"But five billions!" voices from both the right and the left might interrupt.

"Unfortunately we are now left no choice. We have no army except the one created by the present masters of Germany, and the enemy stands without our gates. We cannot on the instant replace William II.'s army by a people's militia, and once this is so, we cannot refuse food, clothing and materials of war to the army that is defending us, no matter how it may be constituted. We are neither repudiating our past nor renouncing our future. We are forced to vote for the war credits."

That would have been about the most convincing thing that Haase could have said.

Yet, even though such considerations might give an explanation of why the Socialist workers as *citizens* did not obstruct the military organization, but simply fulfilled the duty of citizenship forced upon them by circumstances, we should still be waiting in vain for an answer to the principal question: Why did the Social

Democracy, as the political organization of a class that has been denied a share in the government, as the implacable enemy of bourgeois society, as the republican party, as a branch of the International--why did it take upon itself the responsibility for acts undertaken by its irreconcilable class enemies?

If it is impossible for us immediately to replace the Hohenzollern army with a militia, that does not mean that we must now take upon ourselves the responsibility for the doings of that army. If in times of peaceful normal state-housekeeping we wage war against the monarchy, the bourgeoisie and militarism, and are under obligations to the masses to carry on that war with the whole weight of our authority, then we commit the greatest crime against our future when we put this authority at the disposal of the monarchy, the bourgeoisie and militarism at the very moment when these break out into the terrible, anti-social and barbaric methods of war.

Neither the nation nor the state can escape the obligation of defense. But when we refuse the rulers our confidence we by no means rob the bourgeois state of its weapons or its means of defense and even of attack--as long as we are not strong enough to wrest its power from its hands. In war as in peace, we are a party of opposition, not a party of power. In that way we can also most surely serve that part of our task which war outlines so sharply, the work of national independence. The Social Democracy cannot let the fate of any nation, whether its own or another nation, depend upon military successes. In throwing upon the capitalist state the responsibility for the method by which it protects its independence, that is, the violation of the independence of other states, the Social Democracy lays the cornerstone of true national independence in the consciousness of the masses of all nations. By preserving and developing the international solidarity of the workers, we secure the independence of the nation--and make it independent of the calibre of cannons.

If Czarism is a danger to Germany's independence, there is only one way that promises success in warding off this danger, and that way lies with us--the solidarity of the working masses of Germany and Russia. But such solidarity would undermine the policy that William II. explained in saying that the entire German people stood behind him. What should we Russian Socialists say to the Russian workingmen in face of the fact that the bullets the German workers are shooting at them bear the political and moral seal of the German Social Democracy? "We cannot make our policy for Russia, we make it for Germany," was the answer given me by one of the most respected functionaries of the German party when I put this question to him. And at that moment I felt with particularly painful clearness what a blow had been struck at the International from within.

The situation, it is plain, is not improved if the Socialist parties of *both* warring countries throw in their fate with the fate of their governments, as in Germany and France. No outside power, no confiscation or destruction of Socialist property, no arrests and imprisonments could have dealt such a blow to the International as it struck itself with its own hands in surrendering to the Moloch of state just when he began to talk in terms of blood and iron.

*   *   *   *   *

In his speech at the convention at Essen Kautsky drew a terrifying picture of brother rising against brother in the name of a "war of defense"--as an argument, by no means as an actual possibility. Now that this picture has become a bloody actuality, Kautsky endeavors to reconcile us to it. He beholds no collapse of the International.

> "The difference between the German and the French Social-ists is not to be found in their standards of judgment, nor in their fundamental point of view, but merely in the difference of their interpretation of the present situation, which, in its turn, is conditioned by the *difference in their geographical position* [!]. Therefore, this difference can scarcely be overcome while the war lasts. Nevertheless it is not a difference of principle, but one arising out of a particular situation, and so it need not last after that situation has ceased to exist." (*Neue Zeit*, 337, p. 3.)

When Guèsde and Sembat appear as aides to Poincaré, Delcassé and Briand, and as opponents to Bethmann-Hollweg; when the French and German workingmen cut each other's throats and are not doing so as enforced citizens of the bourgeois republic and the Hohenzollern Monarchy, but as Socialists performing their duty under the spiritual leadership of their parties, this is not a collapse of the International. The "standard of judgment" is one and the same for the German Socialist cutting a Frenchman's throat as for the French Socialist cutting a German's throat. If Ludwig Frank takes up his gun, not to proclaim the "difference of principle" to the French Socialists, but to shoot them in all agreement of principle; and if Ludwig Frank should himself fall by a French bullet--fired possibly by a comrade--that is no detriment to "standards" they have in common. It is merely a consequence of the "difference in their geographical position." Truly, it is bitter to read such lines, but doubly bitter when they come from Kautsky's pen.

The International was opposed to the war.

> "If, in spite of the efforts of the Social Democracy, we should have war," says Kautsky, "then every nation must save its skin as best it can. This means for the Social Democracy of every country the same right and the same duty to participate in its country's defense, and none of them may make of this a cause for casting reproaches [!] at each other." (*Neue Zeit*, 337, p. 7.)

Of such sort is this common standard to save one's own skin, to break one another's skulls in self-defense, and not to "reproach" one another for doing so.

But will the question be answered by the *agreement* in the standard of judgment? Will it not rather be answered by the *quality* of this common standard of judgment? Among Bethmann-Hollweg, Sasonov, Grey and Delcassé you also find agreement in their standards. Nor is there any difference of principle between them either. They least of all have any right to cast reproaches at each other. Their conduct simply springs from "a difference in their geographical position." Had Bethmann-Hollweg been an English minister, he would have acted exactly as did

Sir Edward Grey. Their standards are as like each other as their cannon, which differ in nothing but their calibre. But the question for us is, can we adopt *their* standards for *our own*?

> "Fortunately, it is a misconception to assume that the German Social Democracy in case of war wanted to judge by national and not by international considerations, and felt itself to be first a German and then a proletariat party."

So said Kautsky in Essen. And now when the national point of view has taken hold of all the workingmen's parties of the International in place of the international point of view that they held in common, Kautsky not only reconciles himself to this "misconception," but even tries to find in it agreement of standards and a guarantee of the rebirth of the International.

> "In every national state the working class must also devote its entire energy to keeping intact the independence and the integrity of the national territory. This is an essential of democracy, that basis necessary to the struggle and the final victory of the proletariat." (*Neue Zeit*, 337, p. 4.)

But if this is the case, how about the Austrian Social Democracy? Must it, too, devote its entire energy to the preservation of the non-national and anti-national Austro-Hungarian Monarchy? And the German Social Democracy? By amalgamating itself politically with the German army, it not only helps to preserve the Austro-Hungarian national chaos, but also facilitates the destruction of Germany's national unity. *National unity is endangered not only by defeat but also by victory.*

From the standpoint of the European proletariat it is equally harmful whether a slice of French territory is gobbled up by Germany, or whether France gobbles up a slice of German territory. Moreover the preservation of the European *status quo* is not a thing at all for our platform. The political map of Europe has been drawn by the point of the bayonet, at every frontier passing over the living bodies of the nations. If the Social Democracy assists its national (or anti-national) governments with all its energy, it is again leaving it to the power and intelligence of the bayonet to correct the map of Europe. And in tearing the International to pieces, the Social Democracy destroys the one power that is capable of setting up a programme of national independence and democracy in opposition to the activity of the bayonet, and of carrying out this programme in a greater or less degree, quite independently of which of the national bayonets is crowned with victory.

The experience of old is confirmed once again. If the Social Democracy sets national duties above its class duties, it commits the greatest crime not only against Socialism, but also against the interest of the nation as rightly and broadly understood.

CHAPTER VII
THE COLLAPSE OF THE INTERNATIONAL

At their Convention in Paris two weeks before the outbreak of the catastrophe, the French Socialists insisted on pledging all branches of the International to revolutionary action in case of a mobilization. They were thinking chiefly of the German Social Democracy. The radicalism of the French Socialists in matters of foreign policy was rooted not so much in international as national interests. The events of the War have now definitely confirmed what was clear to many then. What the French Socialist Party desired from the sister party in Germany was a certain guarantee for the inviolability of France. They believed that only by thus insuring themselves with the German proletariat could they finally free their own hands for a decisive conflict with national militarism.

The German Social Democracy, for their part, flatly refused to make any such pledge. Bebel showed that if the Socialist parties signed the French resolution, that would not necessarily enable them to keep their pledge when the decisive moment came. Now there is little room for doubt that Bebel was right. As events have repeatedly proved, a period of mobilization almost completely cripples the Socialist Party, or at least precludes the possibility of decisive moves. Once mobilization is declared, the Social Democracy finds itself face to face with the concentrated power of the Government, which is supported by a powerful military apparatus that is ready to crush all obstacles in its path and has the unqualified co-operation of all bourgeois parties and institutions.

And of no less importance is the fact that mobilization wakes up and brings to their feet those elements of the people whose social significance is slight and who play little or no political part in times of peace. Hundreds of thousands, nay millions of petty hand-workers, of hobo-proletarians (the riff-raff of the workers), of small farmers and agricultural laborers are drawn into the ranks of the army and put into a uniform, in which each one of these men stands for just as much as the class-conscious workingman. They and their families are forcibly torn from their dull unthinking indifference and given an interest in the fate of their country. Mobilization and the declaration of war awaken fresh expectations in these circles whom our agitation practically does not reach and whom, under ordinary circumstances, it will never enlist. Confused hopes of a change in present conditions, of a change for the better, fill the hearts of these masses dragged out of the apathy of misery and servitude. The same thing happens as at the beginning of a revolution, but with one all-important difference. A revolution links these newly aroused elements with the revolutionary class, but war links them--with the government and the army! In the one case all the unsatisfied needs, all the accumulated suffering, all the hopes and longings find their expression in revolutionary enthusiasm; in the other case these same social emotions temporarily take the form of patriotic intoxication. Wide circles of the working class, even among those touched with Socialism, are carried along in the same current. The advance guard of the Social Democracy feels it is in the minority; its organizations, in order to complete the organization of the army, are wrecked. Under such conditions there can be no thought of a revolutionary move on the part of the Party. And all this is quite independent of whether the people look upon a particular war with favor or disfavor. In spite of the colonial character of the Russo-Japanese war and its unpopularity in Russia, the first half year of it nearly smothered the revolutionary movement. Consequently it is quite clear that, with the best intentions in the world, the Socialist parties cannot pledge themselves to obstructionist action at the time of mobilization, at a time, that is, when Socialism is more than ever politically isolated.

And therefore there is nothing particularly unexpected or discouraging in the fact that the working-class parties did not oppose military mobilization with their own revolutionary mobilization. Had the Socialists limited themselves to expressing condemnation of the present war, had they declined all responsibility for it and refused the vote of confidence in their governments as well as the vote for the war credits, they would have done their duty at the time. They would have taken up a position of waiting, the oppositional character of which would have been perfectly clear to the government as well as to the people. Further action would have been determined by the march of events and by those changes which the events of a war must produce on the people's consciousness. The ties binding the International together would have been preserved, the banner of Socialism would have been unstained. Although weakened for the moment, the Social Democracy would have preserved a free hand for a decisive interference in affairs as soon as the change in the feelings of the working masses came about. And it is safe to assert that whatever influence the Social Democracy might have lost by such an attitude at the beginning of the war, would have been won several times over once the inevitable turn in public sentiment had come about.

But if this did not happen, if the signal for war mobilization was also the signal for the fall of the International, if the national labor parties fell in line with their governments and the armies without a single protest, then there must be deep causes for it common to the entire International. It would be futile to seek these causes in the mistakes of individuals, in the narrowness of leaders and party committees. They must be sought in the conditions of the epoch in which the Socialist International first came into being and developed. Not that the unreliability of the leaders or the bewildered incompetence of the Executive Committees should ever be justified. By no means. But these are not fundamental factors. These must be sought in the historical conditions of an entire epoch. For it is not a question--and we must be very straightforward with ourselves about this--of any particular mistake, not of any opportunist steps, not of any awkward statements in the various parliaments, not of the vote for the budget cast by the Social Democrats of the Grand Duchy of Baden, not of individual experiments of French ministerialism, not of the making or unmaking of this or that Socialist's career. It is nothing less than the complete failure of the International in the most responsible historical epoch, for which all the previous achievements of Socialism can be considered merely as a preparation.

A review of historical events will reveal a number of facts and symptoms that should have aroused disquiet as to the depth and solidity of Internationalism in the labor movement.

I am not referring to the Austrian Social Democracy. In vain did the Russian and Servian Socialists look for clippings from articles on world politics in the *Wiener Arbeiter Zeitung* that they could use for Russian and Servian workingmen without having to blush for the International. One of the most striking tendencies of this journal always was the defense of Austro-German imperialism not only against the outside enemy but also against the internal enemy--and the *Vorwärts* was one of the internal enemies. There is no irony in saying that in the present crisis of the International the *Wiener Arbeiter Zeitung* remained truest to its past.

French Socialism reveals two extremes--an ardent patriotism, on the one hand, not free from enmity of Germany; on the other hand, the most vivid anti-patriotism of the Hervé type, 'which, as experience teaches, readily turns into the very opposite.

As for England, Hyndman's Tory-tinged patriotism, supplementing his sectarian radicalism, has often caused the International political difficulties.

It was in a far less degree that nationalistic symptoms could be detected in the German Social Democracy. To be sure, the opportunism of the South Germans grew up out of the soil of particularism, which was German nationalism in octavo form. But the South Germans were rightly considered the politically unimportant rearguard of the Party. Bebel's promise to shoulder his gun in case of danger did not meet with a single-hearted reception. And when Noske repeated Bebel's expression, he was sharply attacked in the Party press. On the whole the German Social Democracy adhered more strictly to the line of internationalism than any other of the old Socialist parties. But for that very reason it made the sharpest break with its past. To judge by the formal announcements of the Party and the articles in the Socialist press, there is no connection between the Yesterday and To-day of German Socialism.

But it is clear that such a catastrophe could not have occurred had not the conditions for it been prepared in previous times. The fact that two young parties, the Russian and the Servian, remained true to their international duties is by no means a confirmation of the Philistine philosophy, according to which loyalty to principle is a natural expression of immaturity. Yet this fact leads us to seek the causes of the collapse of the Second International in the very conditions of its development that least influenced its younger members.

CHAPTER VIII
SOCIALIST OPPORTUNISM

The Communist Manifesto, written in 1847, closes with the words: "Working-men of all countries, unite!" But this battle cry came too early to become a living actuality at once. The historical order of the day just then was the middle class revolution of 1848. And in this revolution the part that fell to the authors of the Manifesto themselves was not that of leaders of an international proletariat, but of fighters on the extreme left of the national Democracy.

The Revolution of 1848 did not solve a single one of the national problems; it merely revealed them. The counter-revolution, along with the great industrial development that then took place, broke off the thread of the revolutionary movement. Another century of peace went by until recently the antagonisms that had not been removed by the Revolution demanded the intervention of the sword. This time it was not the sword of the Revolution, fallen from the hands of the middle class, but the militaristic sword of war drawn from a dynastic scabbard. The wars of 1859, 1864, 1866, and 1870 created a new Italy and a new Germany. The feudal caste fulfilled, in their own way, the heritage of the Revolution of 1848. The political bankruptcy of the middle class, which expressed itself in this historic interchange of rôles, became a direct stimulus to an independent proletarian movement based on the rapid development of capitalism.

In 1863 Lassalle founded the first political labor union in Germany. In 1864 the first International was formed in London under the guidance of Karl Marx. The closing watch-word of the Manifesto was taken up and used in the first circular issued by the International Association of Workingmen. It is most characteristic for the tendencies of the modern Labor Movement that its first organization had an international character. Nevertheless this organization was an anticipation of the future needs of the movement rather than a real steering instrument in the class-struggle. There was still a wide gulf between the ultimate goal of the International, the communistic revolution, and its immediate activities, which took the form mainly of international co-operation in the chaotic strike movements of the laborers in various countries. Even the founders of the International hoped that the revolutionary march of events would very soon overcome the contradiction between ideology and practice. While the General Council was giving money to aid groups of strikers in England and on the Continent, it was at the same time making classic attempts to harmonize the conduct of the workers in all countries in the field of world politics.

But these endeavors did not as yet have a sufficient material foundation. The activity of the First International coincided with that period of wars which opened the way for capitalistic development in Europe and North America. In spite of its doctrinal and educational importance, the attempts of the International to mingle in world politics must all the more clearly have shown the advanced workingmen of all countries their impotence as against the national class state. The Paris Commune, flaring up out of the war, was the culmination of the First International. Just as the Communist Manifesto was the theoretical anticipation of the modern labor movement, and the First International was the practical anticipation of the labor associations of the world, so the Paris Commune was the revolutionary anticipation of the dictatorship of the proletariat.

But only an anticipation, nothing more. And for that very reason it was clear that it is impossible for the proletariat to overthrow the machinery of state and reconstruct society by nothing but revolutionary improvisations. National states that emerged from the wars created the one real foundation for this historical work, the national foundation. Therefore, the proletariat must go through the school of self-education.

The First International fulfilled its mission of a nursery for the National Socialist Parties. After the Franco-Prussian War and the Paris Commune, the International dragged along a moribund existence for a few years more and in 1872 was transplanted to America, to which various religious, social and other experiments had often wandered before, to die there.

Then began the period of prodigious capitalistic development, on the foundation of the national state. For the Labor Movement this was the period of the gradual gathering of strength, of the development of organization, and of political possibilism.

In England the stormy period of Chartism, that revolutionary awakening of the English proletariat, had completely exhausted itself ten years before the birth of the First International. The repeal of the Corn Laws (1846) and the subsequent industrial prosperity that made England the workshop of the world; the establishment of the ten-hour working day (1847), the increase of emigration from Ireland to America, and the enfranchisement of the workers in the cities (1867), all these circumstances, which considerably improved the lot of the upper strata of the proletariat, led the class movement in England into the peaceful waters of trade unionism and its supplemental liberal labor policies.

The period of possibilism, that is, of the conscious, systematic adaptation to the economic, legal, and state forms of national capitalism began for the English proletariat, the oldest of the brothers, even before the birth of the International, and twenty years earlier than for the continental proletariat. If nevertheless the big English unions joined the International at first, it was only because it afforded them protection against the importation of strike breakers in wage disputes.

The French labor movement recovered but slowly from the loss of blood in the Commune, on the soil of a retarded industrial growth, and in a nationalistic atmosphere of the most noxious greed for "revenge." Wavering between an anarchistic "denial" of the state and a vulgar-democratic capitulation to it, the French proletarian movement developed by adaptation to the social and political framework of the bourgeois republic.

As Marx had already foreseen in 1870, the center of gravity of the Socialist movement shifted to Germany.

After the Franco-Prussian War, united Germany entered upon an era similar to the one England had passed through in the twenty years previous: an era of capitalistic prosperity, of democratic suffrage, of a higher standard of living for the upper strata of the proletariat.

Theoretically the German labor movement marched under the banner of Marxism. Still in its dependence on the conditions of the period, Marxism became for the German proletariat not the algebraic formula of the revolution that it was at the beginning, but the theoretic method for adaptation to a national-capitalistic state crowned with the Prussian helmet. Capitalism, which had achieved a temporary equilibrium, continually revolutionized the economic foundation of national life. To preserve the power that had resulted from the Franco-Prussian War, it was necessary to increase the standing army. The middle class had ceded all its *political* positions to the feudal monarchy, but had intrenched itself all the more energetically in its *economic* positions under the protection of the militaristic police state. The main currents of the last period, covering forty-five years, are: victorious capitalism, militarism erected on a capitalist foundation, a political reaction resulting from the intergrowth of feudal and capitalist classes--a revolutionizing of the economic life, and a complete abandonment of revolutionary methods and traditions in political life. The entire activity of the German Social Democracy was directed towards the awakening of the backward workers, through a systematic fight for their most immediate needs--the gathering of strength, the increase of membership, the filling of the treasury, the development of the press, the conquest of all the positions that presented themselves, their utilization and expansion. This was the great historical work of the awakening and educating of the "unhistorical" class.

The great centralized trade unions of Germany developed in direct dependence upon the development of national industry, adapting themselves to its successes in the home and the foreign markets, and controlling the prices of raw materials and manufactured products. Localized in political districts to adapt itself to the election laws and stretching feelers in all cities and rural communities, the Social Democracy built up the unique structure of the political organization of the German proletariat with its many-branched bureaucratic hierarchy, its one million dues-paying members, its four million voters, ninety-one daily papers and sixty-five Party printing presses. This whole many-sided activity, of immeasurable historical importance, was permeated through and through with the spirit of possibilism.

In forty-five years history did not offer the German proletariat a single opportunity to remove an obstacle by a stormy attack, or to capture any hostile position in a revolutionary advance. As a result of the mutual relation of social forces, it was forced to avoid obstacles or adapt itself to them. In this, Marxism as a theory was a valuable tool for political guidance, but it could not change the opportunist character of the class movement, which in essence was at that time alike in England, France and Germany. For all the undisputed superiority of the German organization, the tactics of the unions were very much the same in Berlin and London. Their chief achievement was the system of tariff treaties. In the political field the difference was much greater and deeper. While the English proletariat were marching under the banner of Liberalism, the German workers formed an independent party with a Socialist platform. Yet this difference does not go nearly as deep in politics as it does in ideologic forms, and the forms of organization.

Through the pressure that English labor exerted on the Liberal Party it achieved certain limited political victories, the extension of suffrage, freedom to unionize, and social legislation. The same was preserved or improved by the German proletariat through its independent party, which it was obliged to form because of the speedy capitulation of German liberalism. And yet this party, while in *principle* fighting the fight for political power, was compelled in actual practice to adapt itself to the ruling power, to protect the labor movement against the blows of this power, and to achieve a few reforms. In other words: on account of the difference in historical traditions and political conditions, the English proletariat adapted itself to the capitalist state through the medium of the Liberal Party; while the German proletariat was forced to form a party of its own to achieve the very same political ends. And the political struggle of the German proletariat in this entire period had the same opportunist character limited by historical conditions as did that of the English proletariat.

The similarity of these two phenomena so different in their forms comes out most clearly in the final results at the close of the period. The English proletariat in the struggle to meet its daily issues was forced to form an independent party of its own, without, however, breaking with its liberal traditions; and the party of the German proletariat, when the War forced upon it the necessity of a decisive choice, gave an answer in the spirit of the national-liberal traditions of the English labor party.

Marxism, of course, was not merely something accidental or insignificant in the German labor movement. Yet there would be no basis for deducing the social-revolutionary character of the Party from its official Marxist ideology.

Ideology is an important, but not a decisive factor in politics. Its rôle is that of waiting on politics. That deep-seated contradiction, which was inherent in the awakening revolutionary class on account of its relation to the feudal-reactionary state, demanded an irreconcilable ideology which would bring the whole movement under the banner of social revolutionary aims. Since historical conditions forced opportunist tactics, the irreconcilability of the proletarian class found expression in the revolutionary formulas of Marxism. Theoretically, Marxism reconciled with perfect success the contradiction between reform and revolution. Yet the process of historical development is something far more involved than theorizing in the realm of pure thought. The fact that the class which was revolutionary in its tendencies was forced for several decades to adapt itself to the monarchical police state, based on the tremendous capitalistic development of the country, in the course of which adaptation an organization of a million members was built up and a labor bureaucracy which led the entire movement was educated--this fact does not cease to exist and does not lose its weighty significance because Marxism anticipated the revolutionary character of the future movement. Only the most naïve ideology could give the same place to this forecast that it does to the political actualities of the German labor movement.

The German Revisionists were influenced in their conduct by the contradiction between the reform practice of the Party and its revolutionary theories. They did not understand that this contradiction is conditioned by temporary, even if long-lasting circumstances and that it can only be overcome by further social development. To them it was a logical contradiction. The mistake of the Revisionists was not that they confirmed the reformistic character of the Party's tactics in the past, but that they wanted to perpetuate reformism theoretically and make it the only method of the proletarian class struggle. Thus, the Revisionists failed to take into account the objective tendencies of capitalistic development, which by deepening class distinctions must lead to the social revolution as the one way to the emancipation of the proletariat. Marxism emerged from this theoretical dispute as the victor all along the line. But revisionism, although defeated on the field of theory, continued to live, drawing sustenance from the actual conduct and the psychology of the whole movement. The critical refutation of revisionism as a theory by no means signified its defeat tactically and psychologically. The parliamentarians, the unionists, the comrades continued to live and to work in the atmosphere of general opportunism, of practical specializing and of nationalistic narrowness. Reformism made its impress even upon the mind of August Bebel, the greatest representative of this period.

The spirit of opportunism must have taken a particularly strong hold on the generation that came into the party in the eighties, in the time of Bismarck's anti-Socialist laws and of oppressive reaction all over Europe. Lacking the apostolic zeal of the generation that was connected with the First International, hindered in its first steps by the power of victorious imperialism, forced to adapt itself to the traps and snares of the anti-Socialist laws, this generation grew up in the spirit of moderation and constitutional distrust of revolution. They are now men of fifty to sixty years old, and they are the very ones who are now at the head of the unions and the political organizations. Reformism is their political psychology, if not also their doctrine. The gradual growing into Socialism--that is the basis of Revisionism--proved to be the most miserable Utopian dream in face of the facts of capitalistic development. But the gradual political growth of the Social Democracy into the mechanism of the national state has turned out to be a tragic actuality--for the entire race.

The Russian Revolution was the first great event to bring a fresh whiff into the stale atmosphere of Europe in the thirty-five years since the Paris Commune. The rapid development of the Russian working class and the unexpected strength of their concentrated revolutionary activity made a great impression on the entire civilized world and gave an impetus everywhere to the sharpening of political differences. In England the Russian Revolution hastened the formation of an independent labor party. In Austria, thanks to special circumstances, it led to universal manhood suffrage. In France the echo of the Russian Revolution took the form of Syndicalism, which gave expression, in inadequate practical and theoretical form, to the awakened revolutionary tendencies of the French proletariat. And in Germany the influence of the Russian Revolution showed itself in the strengthening of the young Left wing of the Party, in the rapprochement of the leading Center to it, and in the isolation of Revisionism. The question of the Prussian franchise, this key to the political position of Junkerdom, took on a keener edge. And the Party adopted in principle the revolutionary method of the general strike. But all this external shaping up proved inadequate to shove the Party on to the road of the political offensive. In accordance with the Party tradition, the turn toward radicalism found expression in discussions and the adoption of resolutions. That was as far as it ever went.

CHAPTER IX

THE DECLINE OF THE REVOLUTIONARY SPIRIT

Six or seven years ago a political ebb-tide everywhere followed upon the revolutionary flood-tide. In Russia the counter-revolution triumphed and began a period of decay for the Russian proletariat both in politics and in the strength of their own organizations. In Austria the thread of achievements started by the working class broke off, social insurance legislation rotted in the government offices, nationalist conflicts began again with renewed vigor in the arena of universal manhood suffrage, weakening and dividing the Social Democracy. In England, the Labor Party, after separating from the Liberal Party, entered into the closest association with it again. In France the Syndicalists passed over to reformist positions. Gustav Hervé changed to the opposite of himself in the shortest time. And in the German Social Democracy the Revisionists lifted their heads, encouraged by history's having given them such a revenge. The South Germans perpetrated their demonstrative vote for the budget. The Marxists were compelled to change from offensive to defensive tactics. The efforts of the Left wing to draw the Party into a more active policy were unsuccessful. The dominating Center swung more and more towards the Right, isolating the radicals. Conservatism, recovering from the blows it received in 1905, triumphed all along the line.

In default of revolutionary activity as well as the possibility for reformist work, the Party spent its entire energy on building up the organization, on gaining new members for the unions and for the Party, on starting new papers and getting new subscribers. Condemned for decades to a policy of opportunist waiting, the Party took up the cult of organization as an end in itself. Never was the spirit of inertia produced by mere routine work so strong in the German Social Democracy as in the years immediately preceding the great catastrophe. And there can be no doubt that the question of the preservation of the organizations, treasuries, People's Houses and printing presses played a mighty important part in the position taken by the fraction in the Reichstag towards the War. "Had we done anything else we would have brought ruin upon our organization and our presses" was the first argument I heard from a leading German comrade.

And how characteristic it is of the opportunistic psychology induced by mere organization work, that out of ninety-one Social Democratic papers not one found it possible to protest against the violation of Belgium. Not one! After the repeal of the anti-Socialist laws, the Party hesitated long before starting its own printing presses, lest these might be confiscated by the government in the event of great happenings. And now that it has its own presses, the Party hierarchy fears every decisive step so as not to afford opportunity for confiscation.

Most eloquent of all is the incident of the *Verwärts* which begged for permission to continue to exist--on the basis of a new programme indefinitely suspending the class conflict. Every friend of the German Social Democracy had a sense of profound pain when he received his issue of the central organ with its humiliating "By Order of Army Headquarters." Had the *Verwärts* remained under interdiction, that would have been an important political fact to which the Party later could have referred with pride. At any rate that would have been far more honorable than to continue to exist with the imprint of the general's boots on its forehead.

But higher than all considerations of policy and the dignity of the Party stood considerations of membership, printing presses, organization. And so the *Verwärts* now lives as two-paged evidence of the unlimited brutality of Junkerdom in Berlin and in Louvain, and of the unlimited opportunism of the German Social Democracy.

The Right wing stood more by its principles, which resulted from political considerations. Wolfgang Heine crassly formulated these principles of German Reformism in an absurd discussion as to whether the Social Democrats should leave the hall of the Reichstag when the members rose to cheer the Emperor's name, or whether they should merely keep their seats. "The creation of a republic in the German Empire is now and for some time to come out of the range of all possibility, so that it is not really a matter for our present policy." The practical results still not yet achieved may be reached, but only through co-operation with the liberal bourgeoisie. "For that reason, not because I am a stickler for form, I have called attention to the fact that parliamentary co-operation will be rendered difficult by demonstrations that needlessly *hurt the feelings* of the majority of the House."

But if a simple infringement of monarchical etiquette was enough to destroy the hope of reformist co-operation with the liberal middle class, then certainly the break with the bourgeois "nation" in the moment of national "danger" would have hindered, for years to come, not only all desired reforms, but also all reformist desires. That attitude that was dictated to the routinists of the Party center by sheer anxiety over the preservation of the organization was supplemented among the Revisionists by political considerations. Their standpoint proved in every respect to be more comprehensive and won the victory all over. The entire Party press is now industriously acclaiming what it once heaped scorn upon, that the present patriotic attitude of the working class will win for them, after the war, the good will of the possessing classes for bringing about reforms.

Therefore, the German Social Democracy did not feel itself, under the stress of these great events, a revolutionary power with tasks far exceeding the question of widening the state's boundaries, a power that does not lose itself for an instant in the nationalistic whirl, but calmly awaits the favorable moment for joining with the other branches of the International in a purposeful interference in the course of events. No, instead of that the German Social Democracy felt itself to be a sort of cumbersome train threatened by hostile cavalry. For that reason it subordinated the entire future of the International to the quite extraneous question of the defense of the frontiers of the class state--because it felt itself first and foremost to be a conservative state within the state.

"Look at Belgium!" cries the *Verwärts* to encourage the workmen-soldiers. The People's Houses there have been changed into army hospitals, the newspapers suppressed, all Party life crushed out.[5] And therefore hold out until the end, "until the decisive victory is ours." In other words, keep on destroying, let the work of your own hands be a terrifying lesson to you. "Look at Belgium," and out of this terror draw courage for renewed destruction.

What has just been said refers not to the German Social Democracy alone, but also to all the older branches of the International that have lived through the history of the last half century.

---

[5] A sentimental correspondent of the *Vorwärts* writes that he was looking for Belgian comrades in the *Maison du Peuple* and found a German army hospital there. And what did the *Vorwärts* correspondent want of his Belgian comrades? *"To win them to the cause of the German people*--just when Brussels itself had been won 'for the cause of the German people!'"

CHAPTER X

WORKING CLASS IMPERIALISM

There is one factor in the collapse of the Second International that is still unclarified. It dwells at the heart of all the events that the Party has passed through.

The dependence of the proletarian class movement, particularly in its economic conflicts, upon the scope and the successes of the imperialistic policy of the state is a question which, as far as I know, has never been discussed in the Socialist press. Nor can I attempt to solve it in the short space of this work. So what I shall say on this point will necessarily be in the nature of a brief review.

The proletariat is deeply interested in the development of the forces of production. The national state created in Europe by the revolutions and wars of the years 1789 to 1870 was the basic type of the economic evolution of the past period. The proletariat contributed by its entire conscious policy to the development of the forces of production on a national foundation. It supported the bourgeoisie in its conflicts with alien enemies for national liberation; also in its conflicts with the monarchy, with feudalism and the church for political democracy. And in the measure in which the bourgeois turned to "law and order," that is, became reactionary, the proletariat assumed the historical task it left uncompleted. In championing a policy of peace, culture and democracy, as against the bourgeoisie, it contributed to the enlargement of the national market, and so gave an impetus to the development of the forces of production.

The proletariat had an equal economic interest in the democratizing and the cultural progress of all other countries in their relation of buyer or seller to its own country. In this resided the most important guarantee for the international solidarity of the proletariat both in so far as final aims and daily policies are concerned. The struggle against the remnants of feudal barbarism, against the boundless demands of militarism, against agrarian duties and indirect taxes was the main object of working-class politics and served, directly and indirectly, to help develop the forces of production. That is the very reason why the great majority of organized labor joined political forces with the Social Democracy. Every hindrance to the development of the forces of production touches the trade unions most closely.

As capitalism passed from a national to an international-imperialistic ground, national production, and with it the economic struggle of the proletariat, came into direct dependence on those conditions of the world-market which are secured by dreadnaughts and cannon. In other words, in contradiction of the fundamental interests of the proletariat taken in their wide historic extent, the immediate trade interests of various strata of the proletariat proved to have a direct dependence upon the successes or the failures of the foreign policies of the governments.

England long before the other countries placed her capitalistic development on the basis of predatory imperialism, and she interested the upper strata of the proletariat in her world dominion. In championing its own class interests, the English proletariat limited itself to exercising pressure on the bourgeois parties which granted it a share in the capitalistic exploitation of other countries. It did not begin an independent policy until England began to lose her position in the world market, pushed aside, among others, by her main rival, Germany.

But with Germany's growth to industrial world-importance, grew the dependence of broad strata of the German proletariat on German imperialism, not materially alone but also ideally. The *Vorwärts* wrote on August 11th that the German workingmen, "counted among the politically intelligent, to whom we have preached the dangers of imperialism for years (although *with very little success*, we must confess)" scold at Italian neutrality like the extremest chauvinists. But that did not prevent the *Vorwärts* from feeding the German workingmen on "national" and "democratic" arguments in justification of the bloody work of imperialism. (Some writers' backbones are as flexible as their pens.)

However, all this does not alter facts. When the decisive moment came, there seemed to be no irreconcilable enmity to imperialistic policies in the consciousness of the German workingmen. On the contrary, they seemed to listen readily to imperialist whisperings veiled in national and democratic phraseology. This is not the first time that Socialistic imperialism reveals itself in the German Social Democracy. Suffice it to recall the fact that at the International Congress in Stuttgart it was the majority of the German delegates, notably the trade unionists, who voted against the Marxist resolution on the colonial policy. The occurrence made a sensation at the time, but its true significance comes out more clearly in the light of present events. Just now the trade union press is linking the cause of the German working class to the work of the Hohenzollern army with more consciousness and matter-of-factness than do the political organs.

As long as capitalism remained on a national basis, the proletariat could not refrain from co-operation in democratizing the political relations and in developing the forces of production through its parliamentary, communal and other activities. The attempts of the anarchists to set up a formal revolutionary agitation in opposition to the political fights of the Social Democracy condemned them to isolation and gradual extinction. But when the capitalist states overstep their national form to become imperialistic world powers, the proletariat cannot oppose this new imperialism. And the reason is the so-called minimal programme which fashioned its policy upon the framework of the national state. When its main concern is for tariff treaties and social legislation, the proletariat is incapable of expending the same energy in fighting imperialism that it did in fighting feudalism. By applying its old methods of the class struggle--the constant adaptation to the movements of the markets--to the changed conditions produced by imperialism, it itself falls into material and ideological dependence on imperialism.

The only way the proletariat can pit its revolutionary force against imperialism is under the banner of Socialism. The working class is powerless against imperialism as long as its great organizations stand by their old opportunist tactics. The working class will be all-powerful against imperialism when it takes to the battlefield of Social Revolution.

The methods of national parliamentary opposition not only fail to produce objective results, but the laboring masses lose all interest in them because they find that their earnings and their very existence are not affected by what is done in parliament. Behind the backs of the parliamentarians imperialism wins its successes in the world market.

The methods of national-parliamentary opposition not only fail to produce practical results, but also cease to make an appeal to the laboring masses, because the workers find that, behind the backs of the parliamentarians, imperialism, by armed force, reduces the wages and the very lives of the workers to ever greater dependence on its successes in the world market.

It was clear to every thinking Socialist that the only way the proletariat could be made to pass from opportunism to Revolution was not by agitation, but by a historical upheaval. But no one foresaw that history would preface this inevitable change of tactics by such a catastrophal collapse of the International. History works with titanic relentlessness. What is the Rheims Cathedral to History? And what a few hundred or thousand political reputations? And what the life or death of hundreds of thousands or of millions?

The proletariat has remained too long in the preparatory school, much longer than its great pioneer fighters thought it would. History took her broom in hand, swept the International of the epigone apart in all directions and led the slow-moving millions into the field where their last illusions are being washed away in blood. A terrible experiment! On its result perhaps hangs the fate of European civilization.

CHAPTER XI
THE REVOLUTIONARY EPOCH

At the close of the last century a heated controversy arose in Germany over the question, What effect does the industrialization of a country produce upon its military power? The reactionary agrarian politicians and writers, like Sehring, Karl Ballod, Georg Hansen and others, argued that the rapid increase of the city populations at the expense of the rural districts positively undermined the foundation of the Empire's military power, and they of course drew from it their patriotic inferences in the spirit of agrarian protectionism. On the other hand Lujo Brentano and his school championed an exactly opposite point of view. They pointed out that economic industrialism not only opened up new financial and technical resources, but also developed in the proletariat the vital force capable of making effective use of all the new means of defense and attack. He quotes authoritative opinions to show that even in the earlier experiences of 1870-71 "the regiments from the preponderantly industrial district of Westphalia were among the very best." And he explains this fact quite correctly by the far greater ability of the industrial worker to find his bearings in new conditions and to adjust himself to them. Now which side is right? The present War proves that Germany, which has made the greatest progress along capitalistic lines, was able to develop the highest military power. And likewise in regard to all the countries drawn into it the War proves what colossal and yet competent energy the working class develops in its warlike activities. It is not the passive horde-like heroism of the peasant masses, welded together by fatalistic submissiveness and religious superstition. It is the individualized spirit of sacrifice, born of inner impulse, ranging itself under the banner of the Idea.

But the Idea under whose banner the armed proletariat now stands, is the Idea of war-crafty nationalism, the deadly enemy of the true interests of the workers. The ruling class showed themselves strong enough to force their Idea upon the proletariat, and the proletariat, in the consciousness of what they were doing, put their intelligence, their enthusiasm and their courage at the service of their class-foes. In this fact is sealed the terrible defeat of Socialism. But it also opens up all possibilities for a final victory of Socialism. There can be no doubt that a class which is capable of displaying such steadfastness and self-sacrifice in a war it considers a "just" one, will be still more capable of developing these qualities when the march of events will give it tasks really worthy of the historical mission of this class.

The epoch of the awakening, the enlightenment and the organization of the working-class revealed that it has tremendous resources of revolutionary energy which found no adequate employment in the daily struggle. The Social Democracy summoned the upper strata of the proletariat into the field, but it also checked their revolutionary energy by adopting the tactics it was obliged to adopt, the tactics of *waiting,* the strategy of letting your opponent exhaust himself. The character of this period was so dull and reactionary that it did not allow the Social Democracy the opportunity to give the proletariat tasks that would have engaged their whole spirit of sacrifice.

Imperialism is now giving them such tasks. And imperialism attained its object by pushing the proletariat into a position of "national defense," which, to the workers, meant the defense of all their hands had created, not only the immense wealth of the nation, but also their own class-organizations, their treasuries, their press, in short, everything they had unwearyingly, painfully struggled for and attained in the course of several decades. Imperialism violently threw society off its balance, destroyed the sluice-gates built by the Social Democracy to regulate the current of proletarian revolutionary energy, and guided this current into its *own* bed.

But this terrific historical experiment, which at one blow broke the back of the Socialist International, carries a deadly danger for bourgeois society itself. The hammer is wrenched out of the worker's hand and a gun put into his hand instead. And the worker, who has been tied down by the machinery of the capitalist system, is suddenly torn from his usual setting and taught to place the aims of society above happiness at home and even life itself.

With the weapon in his hand that he himself has forged, the worker is put in a position where the political destiny of the state is directly dependent upon him. Those who exploited and scorned him in normal times, flatter him now and toady to him. At the same time he comes into intimate contact with the cannon, which Lassalle calls one of the most important ingredients of all constitutions. He crosses the border, takes part in forceful requisitions, and helps in the passing of cities from one party to another. Changes are taking place such as the present generation has never before seen.

Even though the vanguard of the working-class knew in theory that Might is the mother of Right, still their political thinking was completely permeated by the spirit of opportunism, of adaptation to bourgeois legalism. Now they are learning from the teachings of facts to despise this legalism and tear it down. Now dynamic forces are replacing the static forces in their psychology. The great guns are hammering into their heads the idea that if it is impossible to get around an obstacle, it is possible to destroy it. Almost the entire adult male population is going through this school of war, so terrible in its realism, a school which is forming a new human type. Iron necessity is now shaking its fist at all the rules of bourgeois society, at its laws, its morality, its religion. "Necessity knows no law," said the German Chancellor on August 4th. Monarchs walk about in public places calling each other liars in the language of market-women; governments repudiate their solemnly acknowledged obligations, and the national church ties its God to the national cannon like a criminal condemned to hard labor. Is it not clear that all these circumstances must bring about a profound change in the mental attitude of the working-class, curing them radically of the hypnosis of legality in which a period of political stagnation expresses itself?

The possessing classes, to their consternation, will soon have to recognize this change. A working-class that has been through the school of war will feel the need of using the language of force as soon as the first serious obstacle faces them within their own country. "Necessity knows no law" the workers will cry when the attempt is made to hold them back at the command of bourgeois law. And poverty, the terrible poverty that prevails during this war and will continue after its close, will be of a sort to force the masses to violate many a bourgeois law. The general economic exhaustion in Europe will affect the proletariat most immediately and most severely. The state's material resources will be depleted by the war, and the possibility of satisfying the demands of the working-masses will be very limited. This must lead to profound political conflicts, which, ever-widening and deepening, may take on the character of a social revolution, the course and outcome of which no one, of course, can now foresee.

On the other hand, the War with its armies of millions, and its hellish weapons of destruction can exhaust not only society's resources but also the moral forces of the proletariat. If it does not meet inner resistance, this War may last for several years more, with changing fortunes on both sides, until the chief belligerents are completely exhausted. But then the whole fighting energy of the international proletariat, brought to the surface by the bloody conspiracy of imperialism, will be completely consumed in the horrible work of mutual annihilation. The outcome would be that our entire civilization would be set back by many decades. A peace resulting not from the will of the awakened peoples but from the mutual exhaustion of the belligerents, would be like the peace with which the Balkan War was concluded; it would be a Bucharest Peace extended to the whole of Europe.

Such a peace would seek to patch up anew the contradictions, antagonisms and deficiencies that have led to the present War. And with many other things, the Socialist work of two generations would vanish in a sea of blood without leaving a trace behind.

Which of the two prospects is the more probable? This cannot possibly be theoretically determined in advance. The issue depends entirely upon the activity of the vital forces of society--above all upon the revolutionary Social Democracy.

"Immediate cessation of the War" is the watchword under which the Social Democracy can reassemble its scattered ranks, both within the national parties, and in the whole International. The proletariat cannot make its will to peace dependent upon the strategic considerations of the general staffs. On the contrary, it must oppose its desire for peace to these military considerations. What the warring governments call a struggle for national self-preservation is in reality a mutual national annihilation. Real national self-defense now consists in the struggle for peace.

Such a struggle for peace means for us not only a fight to save humanity's material and cultural possessions from further insane destruction. It is for us primarily a fight to preserve the revolutionary energy of the proletariat.

To assemble the ranks of the proletariat in a fight for peace means again to place the forces of revolutionary Socialism against raging, tearing imperialism on the whole front.

The conditions upon which peace should be concluded--the peace of the peoples themselves, and not the reconciliation of the diplomats--must be the same for the whole International.

NO CONTRIBUTIONS.
THE RIGHT OF EVERY NATION
TO SELF-DETERMINATION.
THE UNITED STATES OF
EUROPE--WITHOUT MONARCHIES,
WITHOUT STANDING ARMIES,
WITHOUT RULING FEUDAL
CASTES, WITHOUT SECRET DIPLOMACY.

The peace agitation, which must be conducted simultaneously with all the means now at the disposal of the Social Democracy as well as those which, with a good will, it could acquire, will not only tear the workers out of their nationalistic hypnosis; it will also do the saving work of inner purification in the present official parties of the proletariat. The national Revisionists and the Socialist patriots in the Second International, who have been exploiting the influence that Socialism has acquired over the working masses for national militaristic aims, must be thrust back into the camp of the enemies of the working class by uncompromising revolutionary agitation for peace.

The revolutionary Social Democracy need not fear that it will be isolated, now less than ever. The War is making the most terrible agitation against itself. Every day that the War lasts will bring new masses of people to our banner, if it is an honest banner of peace and democracy. The surest way by which the Social Democracy can isolate the militaristic reaction in Europe and force it to take the offensive is by the slogan of Peace.

*   *   *   *   *

We revolutionary Marxists have no cause for despair. The epoch into which we are now entering will be *our* epoch. Marxism is not defeated. On the contrary: the roar of the cannon in every quarter of Europe heralds the theoretical victory of Marxism. What is left now of the hopes for a "peaceful" development, for a mitigation of capitalist class contrasts, for a regular systematic growth into Socialism?

The Reformists on principle, who hoped to solve the social question by the way of tariff treaties, consumers' leagues, and the parliamentary co-operation of the Social Democracy with the bourgeois parties, are now all resting their hopes on the victory of the "national" arms. They are expecting the possessing classes to show greater willingness to meet the needs of the proletariat because it has proved its patriotism.

This expectation would be positively foolish if there were not hidden behind it another, far less "idealistic" hope--that a military victory would create for the bourgeoisie a broader imperialistic field for enriching itself at the expense of the bourgeoisie of other countries, and would enable it to share some of the booty with its own proletariat at the expense of the proletariat of other countries. *Socialist reformism has actually turned into Socialist imperialism.*

We have witnessed with our own eyes the pathetic bankruptcy of the hopes of a peaceful growth of proletarian well-being. The Reformists, contrary to their own doctrine, were forced to resort to violence in order to find their way out of the political *cul-de-sac*--and not the violence of the peoples against the ruling classes, but the military violence of the ruling classes against other nations. Since 1848 the German bourgeoisie has renounced revolutionary methods for solving its problems. They left it to the feudal class to solve their own bourgeois questions by the method of war. Social development confronted the proletariat with the problem of revolution. Evading revolution, the Reformists were forced to go through the same process of historical decline as the liberal bourgeoisie. The Reformists also left it to their ruling classes, that is the same feudal caste, to solve the proletarian problem by the method of war. But this ends the analogy.

The creation of national states did really solve the bourgeois problem for a long period, and the long series of colonial wars coming after 1871 finished off the period by broadening the arena of the development of the capitalistic forces. The period of colonial wars carried on by the national states led to the present War of the national states--for colonies. After all the backward portions of the earth had been divided among the capitalist states, there was nothing left for these states except to grab the colonies from each other.

"People ought not to talk," says George Irmer, "as though it were self-evident that the German Empire has come too late for rivalry for world economy and world markets, that the world has already been divided. Has not the earth been divided over and over again in all epochs of history?"

But a re-division of colonies among the capitalist countries does not enlarge the foundation of capitalist development. One country's gain means another country's loss. Accordingly a temporary mitigation of class-conflicts in Germany could only be achieved by an extreme intensification of the class-struggle in France and in England, and *vice versa*. An additional factor of decisive importance is the capitalist awakening in the colonies themselves, to which the present War must give a mighty impetus. Whatever the outcome of this War, the imperialistic basis for European capitalism will not be broadened, but narrowed. The War, therefore, does not solve the labor question on an imperialistic basis, but, on the contrary, it intensifies it, putting this alternative to the capitalist world: *Permanent War or Revolution.*

If the War got beyond the control of the Second International, its immediate consequences will get beyond the control of the bourgeoisie of the entire world. We revolutionary Socialists did not want the War. *But we do not fear it.* We do not give in to despair over the fact that the War broke up the International. History had already disposed of the International.

The revolutionary epoch will create new forms of organization out of the inexhaustible resources of proletarian Socialism, new forms that will be equal to the greatness of the new tasks. To this work we will apply ourselves at once, amid the mad roaring of the machine-guns, the crashing of cathedrals, and the patriotic howling of the capitalist jackals. We will keep our clear minds amid this hellish death music, our undimmed vision. We feel ourselves to be the only creative force of the future. Already there are many of us, more than it may seem. To-morrow there will be more of us than to-day. And the day after to-morrow, millions will rise up under our banner, millions who even now, sixty-seven years after the Communist Manifesto, have nothing to lose but their chains.

Lector House believes that a society develops through a two-fold approach of continuous learning and adaptation, which is derived from the study of classic literary works spread across the historic timeline of literature records. Therefore, we aim at reviving, repairing and redeveloping all those inaccessible or damaged but historically as well as culturally important literature across subjects so that the future generations may have an opportunity to study and learn from past works to embark upon a journey of creating a better future.

This book is a result of an effort made by Lector House towards making a contribution to the preservation and repair of original ancient works which might hold historical significance to the approach of continuous learning across subjects.

HAPPY READING & LEARNING!

LECTOR HOUSE LLP
E-MAIL: lectorpublishing@gmail.com